Contents

Stitch
at
Home

Mandy Shaw

D&C

David and Charles

Introduction

When I was asked by my publishers to write a follow up book to my first, I wondered where I would find the inspiration from, as I had put my heart and soul into *Stitch with Love* and doubted that I could better it. But slowly, then overwhelmingly, the idea of the house and, more importantly, the home came to me.

I am very proud to say I am a homemaker first and foremost, then a maker of all things lovely, which includes my children of course! My need to nurture and protect extends to the family pets – chickens, dog and cats – so once I had decided on my theme, I had plenty of inspiration for my designs.

The very first project in this collection is a stitchery sampler that features almost all the embroidery stitches I have used. This is a great piece to begin with, as it serves to remind you of all the stitches I introduced you to in *Stitch with Love*. However I want to move you on to bigger and greater things, so the emphasis this

time is on appliqué – the application of fabric to create decorative designs; but don't worry, there is plenty of opportunity to use embroidery to embellish the appliqué motifs!

From a sewing machine cover based on my dream craft shop to a sweet little gingerbread house that reminds me of all the happy Christmases spent with family and friends over the years, it is my sincere hope that my designs will resonate with you and your loved ones. The beautiful patchwork quilt is a culmination of the 'home' theme and the houses found there accommodate us all – people, rabbit, dog and chickens – quite nicely.

I hope that my appliqué designs will inspire you: use them to make the projects with me, or use them to adorn your own hand-made ideas. It's all about making, creating and having fun, and passing skills and ideas onto other generations, to friends, family and neighbours. So why wait? Let's get stitching!

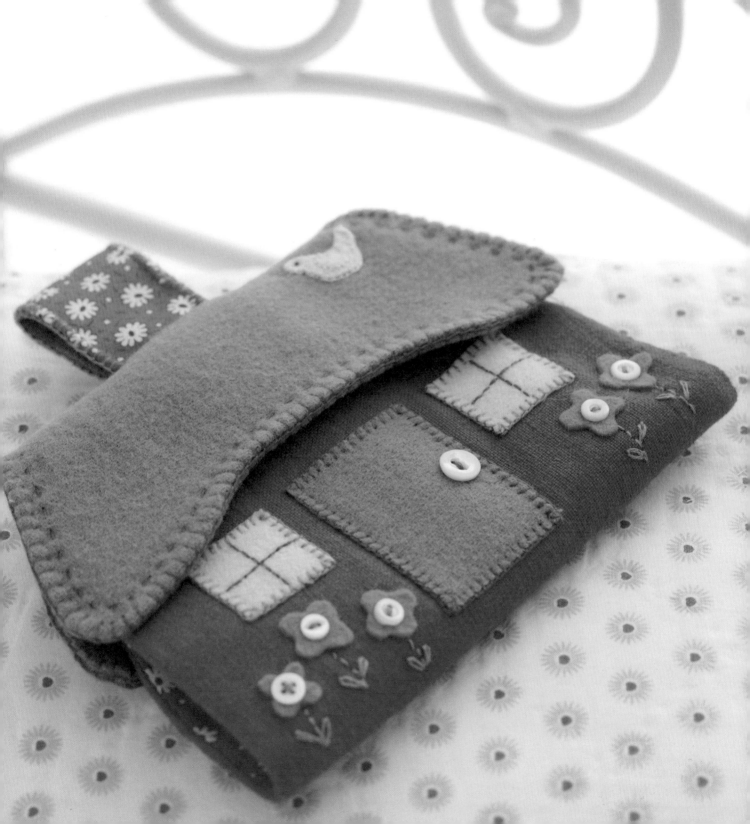

Get Ready to Stitch

Most of the projects in this book are decorated with appliqué embellished with simple embroidery stitches. Appliqué is an easy technique using fusible webbing, but I love to be creative, and I just can't help adding those special little touches with extra hand-worked embroidery stitches and the addition of the occasional button or charm.

Blanket stitch is my favourite appliqué stitch, which can be done by hand or by machine, and even if you choose to machine stitch you can still achieve a hand-stitched look with clever thread selection. This is just one of the secrets I share with you in this chapter, and my aim is to help you to get the best results for your appliqué and embroidery.

Fabrics and Threads

I had such fun finding fabrics to use in this book. I decided on a colour palette of teal, raspberry, brown and cream, and, as dots are in such favour, I opted for those in all different sizes, with some beloved stripes and florals of course.

Linens and cottons

I love to work with 100% cotton and cotton/linen mixes (50/50) to give a clean, crisp textured look to my makes. It is advisable to wash and press your fabrics before you sew in case the colour runs. Fabrics are often treated with a sort of starch dressing to make them easier to sew; after washing and drying your fabrics, you may find that giving them a little spray starch will aid sewing.

Felt

For the best and long-lasting results, use a wool felt or a wool/mix felt at the very least.

Oilcloth

Oilcloth is a waterproof material made by treating one side of a cotton fabric with a synthetic resin. It is not difficult to sew when working from the wrong side of the fabric; when working from the treated side, use a Teflon-coated foot, specially-designed to prevent the machine foot from sticking on the fabric. Alternatively, use your walking foot and help ease the fabric through. Always use a new, sharp, larger-than-normal needle (16/100). Never pin oilcloth as it will leave holes in the fabric, and do not iron it directly as it will melt.

Buttons and braids

I love to to embellish my projects with decorative tapes and pretty buttons, and ric-rac braid is a particular favourite. It can be sewn on by machine or by hand. However, there are a few pitfalls, so do refer to the instructions for working in the Techniques section.

Use a fabric spray adhesive, such as 505, to attach wadding to your material. Follow the manufacturer's instructions and always spray the wadding not the fabric.

Embroidery threads

As the projects call for different styles of stitching, I have used different types of embroidery thread. Stranded cotton (floss) is good for fine work but can be used to embroider thicker lines too, while coton à broder is sometimes too thick for the detailed work required on some projects, so mix and match as you choose.

Coton à broder

A favourite of mine, this single strand thread has a matt finish. It is available in different widths in several colours. I prefer No.16 which is quite thick and ideal for blanket stitching, outlining, backstitching, and quilting. Shops rarely stock the whole range but they can be ordered.

Stranded cotton (floss)

This is available in skeins consisting of six strands which can be pulled out individually for use. It is most usual to use two strands in the needle, but for fine detail use just one, and for a chunkier stitching line use three or more.

Sewing threads

When making up your projects, always use a good-quality sewing thread in a colour to match your chosen fabrics.

Maderia Lana

This is a machine sewing thread that looks like wool and sews up a treat to give a hand blanket stitch appearance. You will need to use a larger size 16/100 needle; make sure you use a good-quality one as cheaper needles may have burrs that will shred the thread. For the bobbin thread, use an ordinary thread. Maderia Lana can also be used to hand quilt and embroider, and you will need to use a large-eyed, good-quality needle.

Needles

Invest in a pack of good-quality mixed embroidery needles. These have large eyes and are very sharp, piercing the fabric and allowing the thread to be pulled through with very little friction. How do you know what size needle to use? If after three attempts the needle won't thread, change to one with a larger hole.

Working the Appliqué

Appliqué takes its name from the French verb *appliquer*, meaning to apply. The technique involves cutting fabric to shape and attaching it to a background fabric to create a surface decoration. The fabric shapes are held in position with fusible webbing and secured and embellished with hand or machine stitching.

Working with fusible webbing

Fusible webbing is an iron-on fabric adhesive that can be purchased in a roll or in pre-cut pieces and it looks like paper. One side is paper-backed and can be drawn on (so you can trace the motif you want) and the other has a thin membrane of glue that melts when heated by an iron to attach it to fabric. It is easy to use if you follow these simple step-by-step instructions.

1. Trace the motif you want onto the paper (smooth) side of the fusible webbing. Cut roughly around the drawn motif rather than following the drawn line accurately at this stage.

2. Iron the fusible webbing onto the wrong side of the appliqué fabric making sure that the fusible webbing is glue (rough) side down. The glue on the back of the fusible webbing melts when heated so be very careful to iron the paper side or else it will stick to your iron.

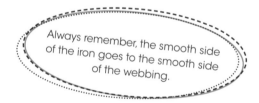

Always remember, the smooth side of the iron goes to the smooth side of the webbing.

3. Once the fusible webbing has been attached to the appliqué fabric you can cut out the motif accurately on the drawn line.

4. Carefully peel off the backing paper and position the appliqué motif onto the fabric it is to be applied to. Iron to fix in place.

5. Always cover the edge of the appliqué with a stitch to seal the edges. This can either be done by hand or by machine.

Many templates provided for the project appliqués are drawn in reverse (like the dog from the Sewing Machine Cover) so that they will be the right way round when you come to fuse and sew them.

Types of fusible webbing

There are several different types of fusible webbing on the market. Here is my guide to the brands you are most likely to encounter. Whichever you choose, always take the time to read the manufacturer's instructions before using.

Bondaweb A fine brand that sews through really well, but in storage the fusible film has a tendency to peel off the paper, so only buy sufficient for each project. A hot steam iron is used to fix the adhesive.

HeatnBond Lite The adhesive film on this product is a little thicker than Bondaweb, so it stores really well. It fixes with a silk setting and if you use a hot iron by mistake it will render the adhesive useless, so take care.

Lite Steam-a-Seam 2 This product has the ability to stick your appliqué in place temporarily until you are ready to iron it, so no pieces of appliqué will come flying off on your journey to the iron.

Tips for machine appliqué

🏠 Always start by giving your machine a little spring clean and a new needle. For best results use a sharp denim variety size 12/80 or 14/90.

🏠 Reduce your top tension a little – you need the top threads to show underneath the work so that no bobbin thread shows on the top. Practise on identical fabric and layers first.

🏠 Use bobbin fill or ordinary thread in the bobbin, and if you have a hole in the arm of your bobbin case, thread your cotton through it to give a better tension.

🏠 If you have a needle-down facility on your machine, use it, as this will help to prevent the stitches from slipping.

🏠 If you have a knee lift, operate it – it will allow you to keep your hands free to manoeuvre your work.

🏠 Use an open-toed embroidery/appliqué presser foot that has a cut-away on the underside – this allows the raised stitch of the appliqué to go under the foot more freely.

🏠 Always start by pulling thread up to the top, sew a couple of stitches on top of each other and then cut the thread. This prevents the threads tangling underneath.

🏠 On curves, stop on the outside edge needle down, raise the presser foot and turn the fabric – stop and start as necessary.

If you overlap adjoining pieces of appliqué you will have only one edge to sew instead of two. For example, on the hen house (Patchwork Quilt) the legs and the house are tucked under the base strip and the roof is placed slightly over the house, so only the base strip and the roof need to be sewn to secure.

Before ironing the appliqué design in place, lay out the individual pieces to help you to establish the fusing order. For example, in the case of the dog kennel (Patchwork Quilt) the inside of the kennel and then the blanket are laid down first, then the kennel is laid on top, and finally the roof and the bone are fused in place.

When fusing fabric strips for roofs, windows and doors, it is easier to cut up pre-fused fabric than use templates, and allows for greater variety to the finished design; while the roof strips used above are the same size, the eaves are cut at different angles and lengths.

Working the Stitches

It's amazing how a little embroidery can lift a design to make it even more interesting. I have included my favourite stitches here, with working instructions for both left- and right-handed sewers. If you are looking to refresh your embroidery skills, the first project in this book, the Sampler Picture, uses almost all of the stitches.

Transferring the embroidery designs

When transferring an embroidery design onto a cream background as for the Sampler Picture and the corner shop window display on the Patchwork Quilt, you should be able to see through the fabric to trace off the design with a fine pencil. Alternatively, use a window as a 'light box' – tape the design to the window, tape your fabric on top and trace off using a pencil, fade away pen or other suitable marker.

Starting and finishing stitching

⌂ Thread your needle – never use more than a short arm's length of thread at one time as it will be more prone to knotting, and more vulnerable to fraying and splitting.

⌂ Start the embroideries with a small knot on the wrong side of the work. To avoid the knot being seen from the front of the work, do keep it small.

⌂ When rejoining a thread, use your needle to weave the new thread into the previous stitches.

⌂ When you have finished your embroidery, weave the thread into the previous sewn work.

⌂ Do not leave long strands hanging on the back as these may show through on the front.

⌂ It is a matter of personal preference as to whether or not you use an embroidery hoop to keep your fabric taut while stitching. I prefer not to as it gets in my way.

SATIN STITCH
A filling stitch used to create a smooth surface decoration.

Right-handers

Work from right to left and take the stitches across from side to side, keeping them even and close; avoid stacking the stitches on top of each other or the effect will be unattractively lumpy. The stitches can be worked in a slanting direction or straight across the design.

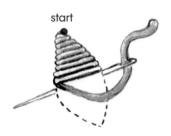

Left-handers

Work from left to right and take the stitches across from side to side, keeping them even and close; avoid stacking the stitches on top of each other or the effect will be unattractively lumpy. The stitches can be worked in a slanting direction or straight across the design.

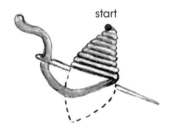

RUNNING STITCH
Run the needle in and out of the fabric for a simple but versatile line stitch.

WHIPPED RUNNING STITCH
Whip a second thread through a line of running stitch for a decorative variation on this simple stitch.

Right-handers

Work from right to left. Bring the needle up through the fabric, make a stitch, and bring the needle down through the fabric again. Repeat, making sure the stitches and the spaces between the stitches are the same size.

Right-handers

Start by sewing the motif with a running stitch. For the best effect, keep the running stitches small. Working from right to left, pull the thread up from behind at the start point and slip the needle over and under one of the running stitches. Continue to whip the thread over in this way until all the running stitches are covered.

Left-handers

Work from left to right. Bring the needle up through the fabric, make a stitch, and bring the needle down through the fabric again. Repeat, making sure the stitches and the spaces between the stitches are the same size.

Left-handers

Start by sewing the motif with a running stitch. For the best effect, keep the running stitches small. Working from left to right, pull the thread up from behind at the start point and slip the needle over and under one of the running stitches. Continue to whip the thread over in this way until all the running stitches are covered.

BACKSTITCH
This is the perfect stitch when a well-defined outline is required.

This stitch may need a little practise to get neat and even. Uneven stitches will still give the desired effect.

Right-handers

Work from right to left. Begin by bringing the needle up a little ahead of where you want the line of stitching to start. Take the needle to the right, to the start position, back through the fabric to make a stitch, and bring it out to the left past the first stitch.

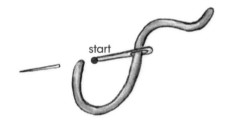

Each time a stitch is made, the thread passes back to fill the gap, for small stitches of an equal length.

Left-handers

Work from left to right. Begin by bringing the needle up a little ahead of where you want to start the stitching. Take the needle to the left, to the start position, back through the fabric to make a stitch, and bring it out to the right past the first stitch.

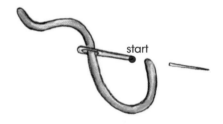

Each time a stitch is made, the thread passes back to fill the gap, for small stitches of an equal length.

BLANKET STITCH
This is a great border or edging stitch.

Aim to keep the length of the stitches even.

Right-handers

Work from left to right. Bring the needle up on the line of the motif or the edge of the appliqué. Take a stitch down from the line and bring the needle back where you started keeping the thread to the left.

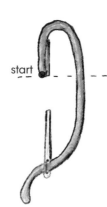

start

Insert the needle to the right of the first stitch, down from the line or edge, and bring it back out on the line or edge, making sure the thread is behind the needle. Pull through.

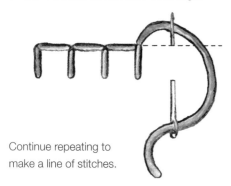

Continue repeating to make a line of stitches.

Left-handers

Work from right to left. Bring the needle up on the line of the motif or the edge of the appliqué. Take a stitch down from the line and bring the needle back where you started keeping the thread to the right.

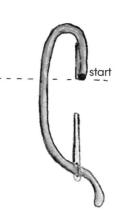

start

Insert the needle to the left of the first stitch, down from the line or edge, and bring it back out on the line or edge, making sure the thread is behind the needle. Pull through.

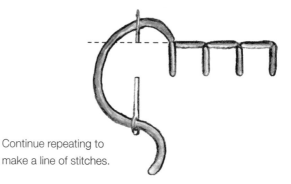

Continue repeating to make a line of stitches.

CHAIN STITCH
A series of looped stitches worked to form a chain-like pattern.

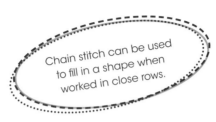

Chain stitch can be used to fill in a shape when worked in close rows.

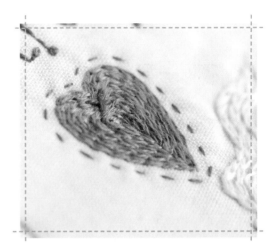

Right-handers

Work from right to left. Bring the needle and thread up at the start point. Holding the thread to the left, put the needle back in where it first came out and bring the needle tip out again a little way beyond this point. Make sure the thread is under the needle and gently pull through.

Left-handers

Work from left to right. Bring the needle and thread up at the start point. Holding the thread to the right, put the needle back in where it first came out and bring the needle tip out again a little way beyond this point. Make sure the thread is under the needle and gently pull through.

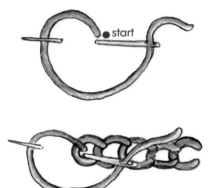

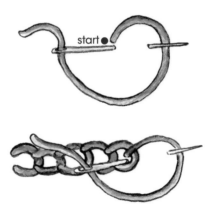

Put the needle in again beside the last stitch and continue. To secure the final stitch, sew a small straight stitch over the final loop.

Put the needle in again beside the last stitch and continue. To secure the final stitch, sew a small straight stitch over the final loop.

LAZY DAISY
A very pretty stitch related to the chain stitch.

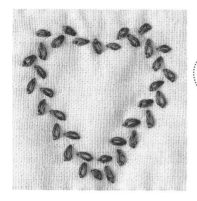

If you pull the stitches tight you get long thin leaves or petals, if you sew them loosely they are plump and fat.

Right-handers

Work from left to right. Bring the needle up through the fabric at the top of the petal, hold the thread down with your thumb. Reinsert the needle at the start point and take it up again at the petal tip, keeping the thread under the needle.

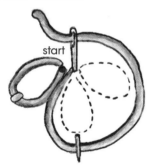

Pull the thread through and, holding the petal down, make a little stitch at the tip to secure.

Left-handers

Work from right to left. Bring the needle up through the fabric at the top of the petal, hold the thread down with your thumb. Reinsert the needle at the start point and take it up again at the petal tip, keeping the thread under the needle.

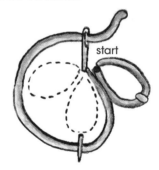

Pull the thread through and, holding the petal down, make a little stitch at the tip to secure.

HERRINGBONE STITCH
A little tricky to get right, but well worth it as this stitch looks great even in small doses.

The motif line runs through the middle of the stitch.

Right-handers

Work from left to right. Bring the needle up below the motif line, cross over to the top right and take a little stitch to the left above the line.

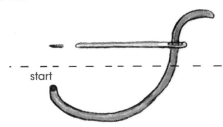

Cross over to the bottom right, and take a little stitch to the left. The needle should come out directly below the stitch above. Continue to line up the top end of a diagonal stitch with the bottom start of another for a nice, even line of stitching.

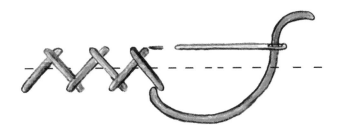

Left-handers

Work from right to left. Bring the needle up below the motif line, cross over to the top left and take a little stitch to the right above the line.

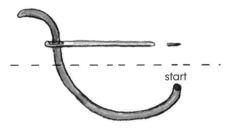

Cross over to the bottom left, and take a little stitch to the right. The needle should come out directly below the stitch above. Continue to line up the top end of a diagonal stitch with the bottom start of another for a nice, even line of stitching.

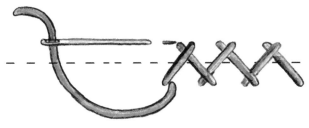

FRENCH KNOT
A useful and cute stitch that must be mastered.

For a larger or smaller knot wrap the thread around the needle more or less times.

Right-handers

Bring the needle up from the back of the fabric, and wrap the thread around the needle two or three times. Put the needle back into the fabric close to where it originally came out. *Do not* go back into the same hole otherwise the knot will be lost.

Left-handers

Bring the needle up from the back of the fabric, and wrap the thread around the needle two or three times. Put the needle back into the fabric close to where it originally came out. *Do not* go back into the same hole otherwise the knot will be lost.

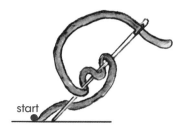

start

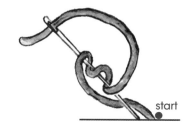

start

Before pulling the needle back through the fabric, gently pull up the thread that is twisted around the needle. Place your fingernail over the twist and pull through.

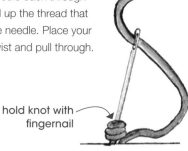

hold knot with fingernail

Before pulling the needle back through the fabric, gently pull up the thread that is twisted around the needle. Place your fingernail over the twist and pull through.

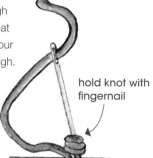

hold knot with fingernail

CROSS STITCH

Most often seen worked in groups, discover the decorative power of the individual cross stitch.

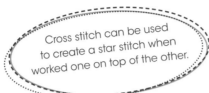

Cross stitch can be used to create a star stitch when worked one on top of the other.

Right-handers

Work from left to right. Bring the needle up through the fabric. Take a stitch diagonally from the top left to the bottom right and bring the needle back out at the lower left corner.

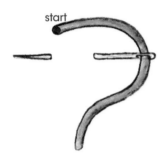

Take a stitch diagonally to the top right corner and bring the needle back where the next cross stitch is required. Pull the needle through to complete the cross stitch.

Left-handers

Work from right to left. Bring the needle up through the fabric. Take a stitch diagonally from the top right to the bottom left and bring the needle back out at the lower right corner.

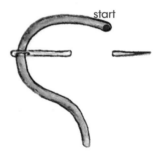

Take a stitch diagonally to the top left corner and bring the needle back out where the next cross stitch is required. Pull the needle through to complete the cross stitch.

Home

I have always adored the lovely old English samplers once worked by young girls as part of their education. The term 'sampler' comes from the Latin *exemplum*, meaning an example to be followed. The patterns these young embroiderers used would often depict pictures of houses and animals and symbols of significance, as well as the alphabet, numbers and improving verses. These were a chance to practise not only their stitching skills, but to learn by rote as they did so. Such samplers now fetch high prices in antiques shops and at auction, so I decided to make my own version inspired by these traditional pieces of textile art.

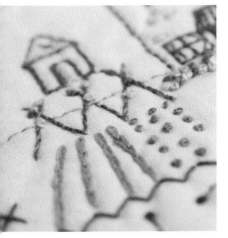

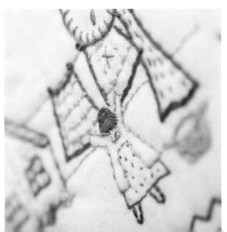

Sampler Picture

My sampler depicts the simple pleasures in life and, just like a traditional sampler, it provides an opportunity to 'sample' almost all the embroidery stitches that are featured in Get Ready to Stitch, with the exception of herringbone stitch.

You will need

- 19cm (7½in) square cream calico
- 2.5cm x 91.5cm (1in x 36in) pink stripe fabric
- 7.5cm x 107cm (3in x 42in) blue dot fabric
- 28cm (11in) square cotton wadding
- Stranded cotton (floss) (Anchor): brown (1086), teal (1064), dark pink (42), pink (36), taupe (392), gold (362), cream (926)
- 28cm (11in) square backing fabric

Finished size: 27cm x 27cm (10½in x 10½in)

Prepare the fabrics

1. Trace the embroidery design (see Templates) centrally onto the calico.

2. Cut four sashing strips from the pink stripe fabric measuring 2.5cm x 20cm (1in x 8in). Fold each piece in half lengthways, wrong sides facing, and press.

3. Taking one strip, place the raw edge along the outer edge of the calico, and tack in place exactly 6mm (¼in) from the folded edge. Repeat with the bottom strip, then each side strip, overlapping at the corners and trimming each end as you go.

4. Cut four border strips from the blue dot fabric, two measuring 5.5cm x 19cm (2¼in x 7½in) and two 5.5cm x 28cm (2¼in x 11in).

5. Place one of the short border strips along one side of the sashing fabric, raw edges matching. Sew in place with an accurate 6mm (¼in) seam and trim the ends. Repeat for the other side, then sew the longer strips along the top and bottom, pressing as you go.

6. Finally, use a spray adhesive to attach the cotton wadding to the back. You are now ready to begin the embroidery.

Embroider the design

note: I choose not to use an embroidery hoop when stitching; use one strand of thread in the needle.

1. To work the alphabet arch, backstitch the letters in dark pink, and add French knot accents in teal. Work the large cross stitches at either end of the arch in brown.

2. To work the number border along the bottom of the design, backstitch in teal, and add French knot accents in dark pink. Chain stitch the hearts at either end in pink, adding a cross stitch to the centre of each in dark pink. Backstitch the zigzag border in dark pink.

3. Fill in the centre heart (beneath the alphabet) with chain stitch in teal; outline in running stitch and add a cross stitch at the top in dark pink.

4. To work the vegetable garden and shed, use taupe to chain stitch the vegetable rows, and teal for the French knot cabbages. Stitch the support canes with a whipped running stitch, using brown for the running stitch and teal to whip. Add a few French knot flowers in dark pink and pink. Chain stitch the shed base in dark pink, filling in the door with gold satin stitch. Backstitch the roof in brown, and add an inner border of gold backstitch and a dark pink cross stitch to finish.

5. For the hanging the washing scene, start by working the outline of the top of the tree with blanket stitch and filling in with lazy daisy 'leaves' in teal. Chain stitch the tree trunk in brown, and fill in with lines of running stitch. Add a dark pink apple in backstitch, with a stem worked in brown. Work the washing line with a taupe backstitch. Outline the two quilts with dark pink backstitch, working the internal lines with pink backstitch. Add a teal cross stitch to the centre of the right-hand quilt. Chain stitch the washing basket in gold. Use satin stitch in brown for the girl's hair and add a French knot bow in dark pink. Backstitch the girl's apron in taupe, her dress in dark pink, and her feet in brown. Decorate the dress with individual stitches in dark pink.

6. For the house, use brown to backstitch the sides of the roof, the roof extension, the porch and the house sides. Use gold backstitch to complete the house sides, and to work the chimney and the feature bricks. Use dark pink backstitch for the windows, and teal backstitch for the curtains. Complete the top and bottom edges of the roof with brown blanket stitch, and fill in with lines of running stitch and cross stitch also worked in brown, with a wavy line of dark pink running stitch in the centre. Infill the front door with chain stitch in teal and satin stitch the door handle in dark pink.

7. For the front garden, work the path outline in gold backstitch and fill in with individual stitches. Work large French knots in an assortment of colours for the flower border along the base of the house. Outline the dog with brown backstitch, and add a teal backstitch collar. Work a large brown French knot for the dog's nose and a smaller one for the eye.

8. For the sky details, backstitch the seagull outline in taupe and work a gold French knot for its beak. Use cream to backstitch the clouds and to chain stitch the smoke from the chimney.

9. Add the 'ground' by working a line of taupe backstitch to either side of the house. This gives the scene dimension.

10. For the decorative flower corners at the top of the design, backstitch the stems in taupe, lazy daisy the flowers in gold and add dark pink French knots for the flower centres.

11. Finally, sew a row of backstitch in dark pink close to the sashing and another row of backstitch in teal approx. 2mm (³⁄₃₂in) in from the dark pink row.

To store your stranded cotton, wind onto an old wooden cotton reel and write the shade number on the top.

Finish the sampler

1. Place the backing fabric on top of the embroidery, right sides together. Pin and tack.

2. Sew along all four sides with a 6mm (¼in) seam, turning the corners very neatly, and leaving a gap in the middle of the bottom seam for turning through.

3. Cut off the excess fabric at the corners and turn the right way out. Push the corners out with a wooden stick to make sure that you get a neat 45-degree angle. Press gently on the back and ladder stitch the opening closed.

4. To quilt the picture, stitch-in-the-ditch between the sashing and the border. The sampler is now ready to be put in a frame of your choosing.

Tea Time

Afternoon tea is a very special event in our house. I am renowned for my cupcakes and chocolate brownies, for my collection of teapots and cake plates, and for my penchant for doilies and cupcake cases. Now you can start your own tea time magic with this striking Union Jack inspired tea cosy and a tablecloth that is ready laid for the occasion.

I have a large family so a six-plate setting is a must for us, but this novelty tablecloth can be easily adapted to suit your own needs. You could even make an individual place setting.

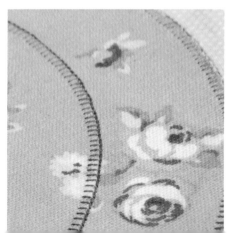

Union Jack Tea Cosy

As afternoon tea is such a great British event, it seems fitting to decorate the centre of the tea table with a very stylish and beautifully practical Union Jack tea cosy. My design is modelled on the national flag of Great Britain, with just a little license with the colours used.

You will need

- 🏠 25.5cm x 66cm (10in x 26in) blue dot fabric
- 🏠 25.5cm x 132cm (10in x 52in) cotton wadding
- 🏠 2.5m (3yd) of 2.5cm (1in) wide cream tape
- 🏠 153cm (60in) dark pink narrow ric-rac
- 🏠 38cm (15in) of 107cm (42in) wide pink stripe fabric
- 🏠 15.5cm x 10cm (6in x 4in) cream felt
- 🏠 5cm x 10cm (2in x 4in) dark pink felt
- 🏠 20cm x 10cm (8in x 4in) fusible webbing
- 🏠 One skein dark pink embroidery thread
- 🏠 158cm (62in) dark pink wide ric-rac
- 🏠 33cm x 79cm (13in x 31in) lining fabric
- 🏠 Two small cream buttons

Finished size: approx. 30.5cm x 20cm (12in x 8in)

Make the front and back

note: the front and the back are made in the same way; make two pieces as follows.

1. Cut a piece of blue dot fabric 32cm x 21.5cm (12½in x 8½in). Cut a piece of cotton wadding the same size.

2. Pin the wadding to the wrong side of the fabric; alternatively lightly spray with spray adhesive and fix in place.

3. Measure and cut two pieces of cream tape long enough to reach from corner to corner across the diagonal. Pin the tape in position and sew in place close to each edge.

4. Pin a length of narrow ric-rac in the centre of each of the diagonal cream tapes, and sew in place straight down the middle.

5. Cut four 6.5cm (2½in) strips across the width of the pink stripe fabric, and put three pieces to one side to use later. Take the fourth strip, and fold and press 6mm (¼in) hems along each long edge. Cut two 32cm (12½in) and two 21.5cm (8½in) lengths from the hemmed strip.

6. Place one of the longer pieces horizontally across the middle of the fabric, and sew in place close to the edges. Place a length of cotton tape, cut to fit, on top; make sure it is centred and again sew in place along its edges. Repeat for a shorter piece of pink stripe fabric, placing it vertically down the middle of the fabric.

7. Cut a simple house shape from half of the cream felt and an elongated heart from half of the dark pink felt. Use the fusible webbing to fix the heart onto the house, and the house onto the middle of the cosy (see Get Ready to Stitch); blanket stitch in place with the dark pink embroidery thread.

8. Using a pencil and a tea plate, mark a curve at the top corners of the decorated fabric piece and trim off.

Join the front and back

1. Join two of the retained 6.5cm (2½in) pink stripe fabric strips together along a short edge.

2. Stitch a line of long running stitch up the long edges of the joined strip, and gather up the strip until it measures approx. 80cm (31in).

3. Pin the wide ric-rac to the edge of the front and back pieces of the tea cosy (but not along the bottom edge), so that the ric-rac humps line up with the raw edge. Tack by hand, or with a large machine stitch, in the middle of the ric-rac.

4. Pin the gathered strip to the edge of one side of the tea cosy with right sides together, pulling up the gathering threads to fit. Sew in place on the ric-rac tacking line to ensure half the humps will be showing. Attach to the other side of the tea cosy in the same way.

Always buy 100% cotton ric-rac as it is easier to sew and will not melt when ironed.

Make the lining

1. Cut a 5cm x 80cm (2in x 31in) strip and two rectangles 20cm x 30.5cm (8in x 12in) from the lining fabric.

2. Using a light application of spray adhesive, attach wadding to the wrong side of the cut fabric pieces and trim to size.

3. Cut off the top corners of the rectangles using a tea plate as a template to match the front and back.

4. Pin the lining strip to the edge of one of the shaped lining pieces (as this will never be seen, there is no need to worry about tucking and pleating) and sew. Repeat for the other side; trim the seams.

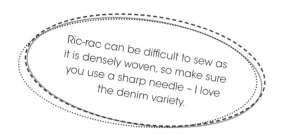

Ric-rac can be difficult to sew as it is densely woven, so make sure you use a sharp needle – I love the denim variety.

Bind and finish

1. Place the lining inside the tea cosy, wrong sides together. Pin the bottom edge well, and trim if necessary.

2. Bind the bottom edge with a 6.5cm (2½in) double binding using the remaining pink stripe fabric strip (see Techniques).

3. To finish, sew a button to the centre of each heart appliqué. This has the added benefit of helping to keep all the layers together.

Place Setting Tablecloth

Use a good quality cotton fabric for your tablecloth so it will wash well, and do a colour-fast test first to make sure the colours of your chosen fabrics do not run. A white cotton sheet would make a great base, dressed up with decorative ribbon tape, bobble trim or ric-rac braid.

You will need

- 🏠 Cotton fabric to fit your table*
- 🏠 Decorative trim**
- 🏠 Fusible webbing
- 🏠 Floral, white dot and dark pink dot fabric for place setting appliqué***
- 🏠 Dinner plate and tea plate for appliqué pattern****
- 🏠 Embroidery threads to match the appliqué fabrics

note: * measure your table top and add an overhang of at least 15.5cm (6in) on all four sides, or longer if you wish; ** measure around the edge of your tablecloth fabric and buy sufficient trim to match; *** quantities will depend on how many place settings you are making; **** I used a 25.5cm (10in) diameter dinner plate and 15.5cm (6in) diameter tea plate for my appliqué pattern, but you could use different sizes if you wish.

Make the tablecloth

1. Hem your chosen tablecloth fabric.

2. Sew a decorative trim around the edges of the hemmed tablecloth as you desire.

Appliqué the place settings

1. First decide how many place settings you require. Put the tablecloth on your table and decide roughly where each will go.

2. Use a dinner plate to cut the number of plates you require from the floral print fabric. For each place setting, cut a spoon, fork and knife blade from white dot fabric, and two fork/spoon handles and one knife handle from the red dot fabric (see Templates).

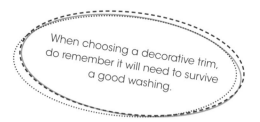

When choosing a decorative trim, do remember it will need to survive a good washing.

3. Working with fusible webbing (see Get Ready to Stitch) and following the photograph opposite, appliqué each plate and cutlery set in place with blanket stitch. Small circles cut from the background of the floral print fabric can be used to 'join' the cutlery handles.

4. Using the smaller tea plate, mark a circle in the middle of the appliqué plate, and blanket stitch around the marked outline.

Sewing

As you may have guessed, sewing is one of the loves of my life. I live and breathe it, so consequently evidence of it is everywhere in my home. However, that large white sewing machine sometimes needs to be disguised, if only for birthday parties and Christmas celebrations, and a lovely dust jacket will do the job nicely. As an added bonus, the doors of this sewing store open to reveal a few essential tools such as threads, needles, marker pencils and ruler. For those occasions when you want to stitch on-the-go, the Cottage Sewing Case provides a handy way to take your stitching tools with you!

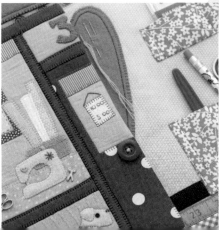

Sewing Machine Cover

My sewing machine is out all the time ready for use but I have designed this attractive cover, which doubles up as useful sewing accessory store, to disguise it.

You will need

For the dust cover

- 63.5cm x 106.5cm (25in x 42in) teal large dot (main) fabric
- 28cm x 106.5cm (11in x 42in) brown (roof) fabric
- 1m (39¼in) of 106.5cm (42in) wide teal small dot (lining) fabric*
- 1m (39¼in) cotton wadding
- 158cm (62in) brown medium ric-rac
- 158cm (62in) of 5cm (2in) wide ready-made binding

For the appliqué storage compartment

- 20cm x 50cm (8in x 20in) heavy-weight interfacing
- 25.5cm x 61cm (10in x 24in) cream fabric
- 50cm (20in) fusible webbing
- 18cm x 7.5cm (7in x 3in) pink stripe fabric
- 16.5cm x 32cm (6½in x 12½in) teal fabric
- 18cm x 10cm (7in x 4in) teal small dot fabric
- 13cm x 20cm (5in x 8in) dark pink spot fabric
- 50cm x 15.5cm (20in x 6in) brown fabric
- Selection of other fabric and felt for the appliqué**
- 63.5cm x 6.5cm (25in x 2½in) teal felt
- 10cm x 15.5cm (4in x 6in) pink felt
- 18cm x 64cm (7in x 25in) pink floral fabric
- Buttons: two large, two small, one micro and one heart-shaped
- Scissor charms
- Embroidery threads to match fabrics
- 55cm x 45cm (20½in x 17½in) fusible medium-weight interfacing
- 40.5cm (16in) tape measure tape
- Hook-and-loop fastener tape

Finished size: 52cm x 44.5cm (20½in x 17½in)

note: * if you choose not to make the sewing compartment doors, you will not need quite as much lining fabric as this; ** details of the appliqué fabrics used for the shop window decorations are given in the making up instructions, but you can substitute for any fabrics that you have.

Cut the fabric for the storage compartment doors

1. Cut the following:
Two pieces of heavy-weight interfacing, 20cm x 25.cm (8in x 10in);
Two pieces of cream fabric, 25.cm x 30.5cm (10in x 12in);
Two pieces of teal small dot lining fabric, 25.cm x 30.5cm (10in x 12in).

2. Spray glue or tack (baste) the interfacing to the wrong side of the cream fabric.

Appliqué the left-hand door

note: when fusing the appliqué to the cream background fabric, make sure that you keep the seams around the outside edge of the interfacing clear of decoration by about 2.5cm (1in); use the photograph opposite as a positioning guide.

1. Apply fusible webbing to the pink stripe fabric (see Get Ready to Stitch); cut two strips 15.5cm x 2.5cm (6in x 1in) and two strips 4cm x 2.5cm (1½ in x 1in). Along the bottom edge of the longer strips, cut a slightly curvy line. (Set one long and one short strip aside for use on the right-hand door.) Iron the longer strip in place along the top of the shop window for the curtains (the shorter strip will be used a little later for the shop door curtain).

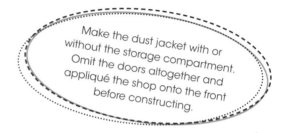

Make the dust jacket with or without the storage compartment. Omit the doors altogether and appliqué the shop onto the front before constructing.

2. Fuse the teal fabric and cut two strips 7.5cm x 16.5cm (3in x 6½in) from it. Set one strip aside for use on the right-hand door and iron the other to the bottom of the shop.

3. Fuse the teal small dot fabric and cut two strips 4cm x 16.5cm (1½in x 6½in). Set one strip aside for use on the right-hand door and iron the other above the teal fabric to create the shop counter, butting it up to the teal fabric.

4. Now move on to create the shop window display. To make the heart quilt, cut a 7.5cm x 5cm (3in x 2in) cream dot rectangle and fuse onto the cream background. Cut the quilt border strips from dark pink small dot fabric, two 1.3cm x 7.5cm (½in x 3in) and two 1.3cm x 5.5cm (½in x 2¼in); fuse in place. Cut a heart from an offcut of teal felt and appliqué to the middle of the quilt to finish.

5. Cut a taupe fabric square and round off the edges to make the fabric basket; appliqué to the display counter. Cut three strips of different fabrics for the fabric rolls and appliqué in place. Blanket stitch along the top of the shop counter. Appliqué a cream felt sewing machine (see Templates) onto the counter overlapping onto the basket.

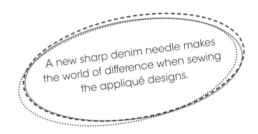

A new sharp denim needle makes the world of difference when sewing the appliqué designs.

6. Using the templates provided, cut the dressmaker's dummy from pink floral fabric and the stand from a taupe fabric; appliqué in place.

7. Now move on to make the shop door. Fuse the dark pink spot fabric and cut into two pieces to give you the two doors. Cut away a window measuring 9cm x 8.2cm (3½in x 3¼in). The window is cut 1.8cm (¾in) in from the top and the side. Appliqué the shorter pink stripe strip in place before ironing the door in place; blanket stitch around the door window frames and the lower inner edge of the doors.

8. Cut a cream 2.5cm (1in) square for the shop sign and appliqué in place on the shop door window. Cut the number 3 from teal felt (see Templates) and appliqué above the door.

9. Cut the dog (see Templates) from cream felt and his scarf from dark pink gingham; appliqué the dog onto the teal fabric (so he is sitting patiently outside the shop).

10. To complete the shop frontage, cut a piece of brown fabric measuring 5cm x 50cm (2in x 20in) and apply fusible webbing to the back of it. Cut the fused fabric into 1.3cm (½in) strips. Cut two 16cm (6¼in) strips for the window sills; set aside one for the right-hand door and appliqué the other in place. Cut two 5.5cm (2¼in) strips for the top of the door frame; set aside one for the right-hand door and appliqué the other in place. Cut two 24.5cm (9¾in) strips for the uprights to complete the door frame; set aside one for the right-hand door and appliqué the other in place. Cut two 21.5cm (8½in) strips for the top of the window frame; set aside one for the right-hand door and appliqué the other in place. Note, the frame at the left-hand edge will be added later.

Appliqué the right-hand door

1. Fuse the set-aside long pink stripe strip to the top of the window and the teal shop front at the base. Fuse the blue small dot shop window display counter in place.

2. Now create the shop window display. Cut two quilt stand posts from taupe fabric, cutting one shorter (see Templates), and appliqué the quilt frame to the right. Cut a quilt border from fused pink gingham fabric measuring 10cm x 13cm (4in x 5in) and cut out the middle section. Cut a quilt top from a fused 10cm (4in) square of white dot fabric; place the quilt top behind the quilt border and appliqué in place. Cut a piece of fused cream fabric 5cm x 3.5cm (2in x 1⅜in) for the sampler picture and appliqué to the left of the quilt.

3. Fuse the set-aside door in place remembering to appliqué the short pink stripe strip in place before ironing the door in place. Cut the number 7 from teal felt (see Templates) and appliqué above the door. Fuse and appliqué the set-aside fused brown strips, starting with the window sill, then the top of the door frame, then the door upright and finally the strip that finishes the window frame. Note, the frame at the right-hand edge will be added later.

Embroider and line the doors

1. Starting with the left-hand door, sew a small round button to the shop front for the dog lead post, and chain stitch the dog lead in dark pink. Sew a micro button (or bead) for the dog's eye and satin stitch the nose in brown.

2. Sew a small heart button to the left of the sewing machine, and embroider a dark pink lazy daisy flower to the right. Satin stitch a pink cotton reel.

3. On the quilt, sew the inner border of backstitch to the teal heart and an outer border of running stitch. Add a running stitch border to the inside of the quilt top.

4. Backstich the shop opening times on the door sign and chain stitch the hanging thread. Finally, sew on the scissor charms.

5. Moving on to the right-hand door, backstitch the lines on the quilt in pink to make the blocks, and embroider on a few houses.

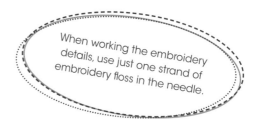

When working the embroidery details, use just one strand of embroidery floss in the needle.

6. Backstitch the heart and houses on the picture in pink, and chain stitch a hanging string. Sew a small button on top of the string.

7. Pin a piece of the teal small dot lining to each door, right sides facing. Stitch along the top, the inner side of the door, and the bottom, close to the interfacing.

8. Trim the seam, cut off the corners and turn the right way out. Push out the corners with a stick and press. Finally, sew on the two large button door handles.

Cut and prepare the dust cover fabrics

1. From the main fabric, cut two pieces 52cm x 32cm (20½in x 12½in) for the front and back and two pieces 27cm x 32cm (10½in x 12½in) for the sides.

2. From the roof fabric, cut two pieces 52cm x 14cm (20½in x 5½in) for the front and back and two pieces 27cm x 14cm (10½in x 5½in) for the sides.

3. From the cotton wadding, cut two pieces 52cm x 45cm (20½in x 17½in) for the front and back and two pieces 27cm x 45cm (10½in x 17½in) for the sides.

4. From the lining fabric, cut two pieces 57.5cm x 45cm (22½in x 17½in) for the front and back and two pieces 27cm x 45cm (12½in x 17½in) for the sides.

5. Place the front roof to the front piece of the main fabric with right sides facing, and sew; press. Repeat for the back and for the sides of the dust cover.

6. Pin a length of ric-rac cut to fit over the seam joining the roof to the house on each of the four sections. Sew in place down the middle of the ric-rac.

Make the sewing accessory storage compartment

1. Iron the medium-weight interfacing to the wrong side of the front of the dust cover.

2. Cut a piece of teal small dot lining fabric 40.5cm x 25.5cm (16in x 10in). Fuse and appliqué to the middle of the front of the dust cover, lining up the bottom edges.

3. Cut a long heart (see Templates) from pink felt and appliqué at the centre top. Topstitch the heart 6mm (¼in) in from the outside edge.

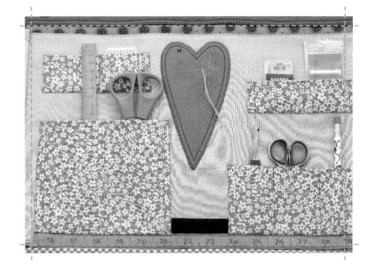

4. Now make the four pockets. First cut the following pink floral fabric pieces: one 16.5cm (6½in) square, one 27cm x 16.5cm (10½in x 6½in), one 14cm x 9cm (5½in x 3½in), and one 14cm x 11.5cm (5½in x 4½in). Fold the fabric right sides together and sew up along the side seams. Cut off the corners, turn the right way out and press. Turn under 6mm (¼in) along the raw edges and press.

5. Place the largest pocket 1.3cm (½in) up from the bottom edge and 1.3cm (½in) in from the side. Topstitch in place. To divide the pocket into two sections, sew a line of machine stitches up the centre.

6. Place one of the small pockets above the large pocket, 4cm (1½in) above and 1.3cm (½in) in from the side. Stitch in place and divide into two as for the large pocket.

7. Sew the medium pocket to the right-hand side 1.3cm (½in) in from the edge, and aligning at the base with the large pocket. Stitch in place as before, but this time sew two dividing lines to make three storage sections.

8. Place the last small pocket 10cm (4in) above the medium pocket, 1.3cm (½in) in from the edge. Now sew the tape measure tape along the bottom edge.

9. To create the shop fascia, fuse and appliqué the teal felt strip onto the main fabric above the storage compartment. Appliqué a felt 'button' to the left-hand side: cut a circle from an offcut of pink felt, sew a backstitch circle within the circle and sew a cross stitch in the middle. Topstitch the fascia 6mm (¼in) in from the outside edge.

Construct and finish the cover

1. Cut two strips of brown fabric 4cm x 27cm (1½in x 10½in); fold in half and press. Turn the ends over by 6mm (¼in) and press.

2. Pin the doors over the storage compartment panel. Place one of the brown strips to the left-hand door, raw edges matching. Pin well and sew with a 6mm (¼in) seam. Turn the strip over to cover the raw edges of the door and machine stitch in place. Attach the remaining brown strip to the right-hand door in the same way.

3. Match up the wadding and lining pieces onto the front, back and sides and lightly spray glue or tack (baste) together, centralizing the wadding in the middle of the lining. (Note: the side linings are bigger than the sides.)

4. Place one side and a front right sides together and sew with a 6mm (¼in) seam, ignoring the over hang of the lining. The extra width of the lining can now be turned over and under, and slip stitched to cover the edges of the seam to make it neat (Fig. 1). Sew the other three seams in exactly the same way to complete the initial stage of the construction.

Fig. 1

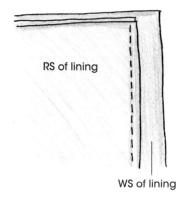
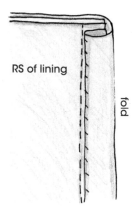

RS of lining

WS of lining

RS of lining

fold

5. Turn the sewing machine cover the right way out. Fold the sides in to the middle at the top edge until the side seams meet (Fig. 2). Pin across the top edge catching in the folds. This forms the roof ridge and will be quite bulky so make sure you pin it well.

Fig. 2

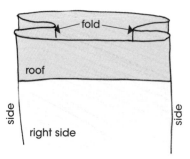

fold

roof

side

right side

side

6. Bind the top edge by cutting a piece of the brown fabric 53cm x 7.5cm (21in x 3in). Fold and press the fabric along its length. Place the binding to the roof ridge, raw edges matching, and turn under each end; pin well and stitch with a 1.3cm (½in) seam. This will be really thick so sew slowly. Turn the binding over to cover the raw edges of the roof ridge and slip stitch in place.

7. Bind the bottom edge of the machine cover with a length of binding measuring 153cm x 5cm (60½in x 2in); for more detail, see Techniques.

8. To keep the doors closed use a little hook-and-loop fastener tape: sew a 5cm (2in) strip between the bottom storage pockets and a 2.5cm (1in) strip on the inside edge of each door to match up.

To personalize the finished dust cover, you could embroider your name on the fascia board.

Cottage Sewing Case

This delightful thatched cottage-shaped sewing case has a vintage feel and is an ideal project for using up your fabric leftovers. It would make a perfect first sewing kit for a little girl, for who wouldn't want to sew with a case like this!

You will need

- 🏠 20cm x 28cm (8in x 11in) thick interfacing
- 🏠 20cm x 28cm (8in x 11in) cotton wadding
- 🏠 23cm x 30.5cm (9in x 12in) floral print cotton
- 🏠 23cm x 30.5cm (9in x 12in) plain cotton
- 🏠 20cm x 25.5cm (8in x 10in) gingham fabric
- 🏠 16.5cm x 43cm (6½in x 17in) teal felt
- 🏠 Cream, teal and rose pink felt offcuts for the appliqué and sewing accessory pockets
- 🏠 13cm (5in) of 5mm (¼in) wide white elastic
- 🏠 Embroidery threads to match fabrics
- 🏠 Several small round and heart-shaped buttons
- 🏠 Three small poppers

Finished size: 20cm x 13cm (8in x 5in) excluding chimney

Prepare the patterns

1. Enlarge all the sewing case patterns (see Patterns) and cut out.

2. You will need to make the house pattern full size. To do so, take a piece of A4 (US letter) sheet of paper and fold in half widthways. Place the house pattern on the piece of folded paper as marked, and trace around it; cut and open out to reveal the full-size house pattern.

Cut and prepare the house

1. Using the full-size house pattern, cut one from the interfacing and one from the cotton wadding the exact size of the pattern. Cut one from the floral print cotton fabric for the lining and one from the plain cotton for the main fabric 2.5cm (1in) bigger all the way around.

2. Using a spray fabric adhesive, lightly spray the interfacing and attach to the cotton wadding. Now lightly spray the wadding and press onto the wrong side of the lining fabric so that it is perfectly centred on the fabric, leaving a 2.5cm (1in) border all around. (Alternatively, tack the layers together.)

3. Fold over the extra fabric at the top and bottom edges and pin in place. Fold in half and mark the centre fold with a pin on the right side.

Cut and prepare the gingham pocket

1. Fold the gingham fabric in half with right sides together. Place the pocket pattern on the folded fabric as marked and cut out.

2. Starting and finishing 1.3cm (½in) down from the folded edge, sew all around the edge of the pocket leaving no gap. Cut a 2.5cm (1in) slit near the bottom of the pocket through one layer of fabric only, and turn the right way out. Press well.

3. To make a channel for the elastic, sew a line of stitching 1.3cm (½in) down from the folded edge; sew a second line just beneath the folded edge. Thread the elastic through the channel using a small safety pin as a 'needle'. Sew one end of the channel closed and snip off the protruding elastic. Pull up the elastic at the other end until the top of the pocket measures 6.5cm (2½in), and secure (this will be neatened later when the felt tags are added).

Cut and prepare the scissor keeper heart

1. Cut out a 7.5cm x 11.5cm (3in x 4½in) rectangle from teal felt offcuts and another from the gingham fabric (for the lining), and place right sides together. Place the scissor keeper heart pattern on top and pin together. DO NOT CUT OUT.

2. Sew with a small stitch along the outline of the heart, through the paper, felt and fabric.

3. Once you have completed sewing the heart shape, tear off the paper and cut out quite close to the sewn edge. Snip the point of the heart and the inner curve to help create a neat shape when it is turned through.

4. Make a small slit in the gingham fabric at the bottom edge of the heart and turn the right way out. Sew the opening closed and press gently. Embroider a row of decorative backstitch 6mm (¼in) in from the edge of the heart.

Sew and finish the gingham pocket

1. Centre the gingham pocket on the inside of the case 1.3cm (½in) up from the centre fold. Machine stitch in place, leaving the elasticized edge open. Decorate the edges with blanket stitch.

2. Using the relevant patterns, cut two pocket side tags and two pocket top tags from teal felt offcuts. Sew the two pocket top tags together with blanket stitch, and attach immediately above the pocket with backstitch. Sew a decorative button on the top side of the other end of the tag and one popper half on the underside. Sew the remaining popper half to the pocket. Blanket stitch the side tags over the ends of the elastic, and sew on two small heart buttons.

Sew and finish the scissor keeper heart and sewing accessory tags

1. Cut one unpicker tag, two thread tags, and two scissor keeper tags from teal felt offcuts.

2. Blanket stitch around the top edge of the heart. Pin the base of the heart 1.3cm (½in) up from the centre fold on the inside of the case, directly opposite the gingham pocket. Continue to blanket stitch the heart onto the lining fabric (leaving the top edge open for inserting the scissors).

3. Sew around the edges of the scissor keeper tag with blanket stitch, and attach the straight end immediately above the heart pocket with a backstitch. Sew a decorative button on the top side of the shaped end and one half of a popper on the underside. Sew the remaining popper half to the heart.

4. Blanket stitch around the unpicker tag and sew in place at each end alongside the heart. Blanket stitch the thread tags together and sew the straight end in place on the other side. On the rounded end, sew a decorative button on the top side and one popper half on the underside. Sew the remaining popper half onto the lining fabric.

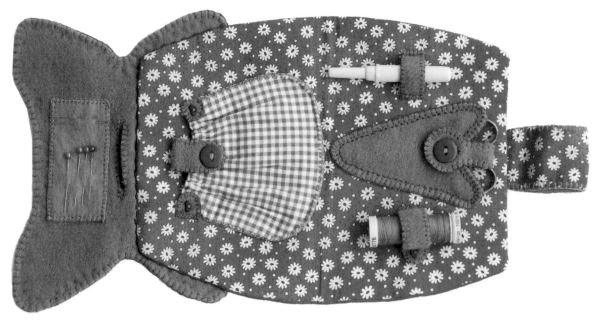

Appliqué and embroider the house front

1. Cut a door measuring 4cm x 5.5cm (1½in x 2¼in) from an offcut of teal felt. Cut two windows from cream felt measuring 3cm x 2.5cm (1⅛in x 1in). Working with fusible webbing (see Get Ready to Stitch), appliqué the door and windows to the remaining plain cotton house piece. Position the door on the middle of the centre fold and line the windows up to the top of the door, 1.3cm (½in) from either side. Decorate the edges with blanket stitch. Divide the windows into four panes using lines of backstitch.

2. Cut out four-petal flowers from rose pink felt and sew in place with small buttons. Embroider with backstitch stems and lazy daisy leaves. Sew a small button handle onto the door.

Sew lining and main fabric together

1. Place the lining and the main fabric right sides together (note, the doors and windows should be on the same side as the scissor keeper heart), and pin well.

2. Sew all the way around the outside edge of the interfacing leaving a 7.5cm (3in) opening directly above the door for turning through. DO NOT SEW ON THE INTERFACING.

3. Trim the seams and corners and turn the right way out. This can be a little fiddly so take your time. (Leave the opening for now; it will be finished later when the chimney is added to the roof.)

Prepare and sew the roof

1. Cut the teal felt into two rectangles measuring 16.5cm x 21.5cm (6½in x 8½in). Place right sides together and pin the roof pattern on top. DO NOT CUT OUT. With a small stitch sew all the way around the outline of the roof, through the paper. Cut out the shaded area in the middle of the template. Now tear off the paper and cut out close to the stitching.

2. Turn the right way out through the slit opening and use a teaspoon to push out the seams. Blanket stitch around the edge of the roof and the slit opening, and sew a running stitch border 6mm (¼in) in from the edge.

3. Pin one half of the roof to the back of the house and slip stitch in place. Cut a rectangle of pink felt measuring 6.5cm x 4cm (2½in x 1½in) and sew onto the inside of the roof flap with blanket stitch to make the needle keeper.

Make the chimney and finish

1. Use the chimney pattern to cut one from the floral print cotton and one from teal felt. Place right sides together and sew a 6mm (¼in) seam along the long edges. Turn the right way out and blanket stitch along the seamed edges. Fold the chimney in half floral side out, and put the raw ends into the opening left when you turned the house the right way out; slip stitch closed with the chimney in the seam. To close the sewing case, thread the chimney through the slit opening in the roof.

2. Cut a bird from cream felt and blanket stitch to the roof, adding a French knot eye.

Pets

Our home has always been full of pets. At present we have Teddy the human dog, Izzy a black cat with attitude, Keith a wrinkly tortoise, Susie, Dolly and Dotty the chickens, Flossie the cockerel, and an assortment of fish. Ted is at the head of the pecking order. He lives under the Welsh dresser with an assortment of toys and an array of gorgeous dog beds. If you want to pamper your pooch, why not make him a bed like Ted's, or a dandy neckerchief that he can wear on his collar. My darling little dog (a West Highland Terrier crossed with a Norfolk) has even inspired a delightful soft toy.

Dog Bed

Ted needs a new dog bed and this is what I have come up with. It is perfect for a medium-sized dog. To ensure that the dog bed can be washed easily, it is a good idea to use an old cotton sheet to make an inner bag for the filling.

You will need

- 50cm (20in) of 150cm (60in) wide main fabric*
- 2.5m (2¾yd) extra wide ric-rac
- 40cm (16in) of 150cm (60in) wide contrasting fabric*
- Blue dot, dark pink and cream fabric offcuts for the appliqué
- Fusible webbing
- Embroidery threads
- 50cm (20in) hook-and-loop fastener tape
- Recycled cotton sheet
- Polystyrene balls for filling

notes: *choose sturdy, washable fabrics – upholstery and denim are great choices; sew 6mm (¼in) seam allowances throughout unless otherwise specified.

Finished size: 68.5cm x 50cm x 15.5cm (27in x 20in x 6in)

Cut and prepare the top and bottom pieces

1. Cut two pieces from the main fabric measuring 68.5cm x 50cm (27in x 20in).

2. Using a large 28cm (11in) diameter dinner plate as a guide, mark a curve with a pencil at each corner of the fabric rectangles. Cut around the marked lines.

3. Sew the ric-rac to the edge of one of the trimmed pieces with right sides facing (see Techniques).

4. Fold each rectangle in half and half again, and mark the fold lines with pins.

Cut and prepare the side pieces

1. Cut two strips from the contrasting fabric, one measuring 16.5cm x 142cm (6½in x 56in) and one 21.5cm x 72cm (8½in x 28½in).

2. Working with fusible webbing (see Get Ready to Stitch), appliqué the kennels onto the narrower, longer strip. Cut five kennels (see Templates, Dog Kennel Block), three from blue dot and two from dark pink fabric, and position around the strip approx. 10cm (4in) apart. Blanket stitch in place.

3. Cut the dog from cream fabric and appliqué to overlap the left-hand edge of the first pink kennel. Secure the dog with cream blanket stitch, and use black thread to satin stitch his nose and add a French knot eye. Use a blue thread to chain stitch on a collar.

You can appliqué small rectangles cut from cream fabric to make little name plates for the dog kennels, and add your dog's name and those of his little doggie friends in backstitch for a fun touch.

5. Join the hook-and-loop fastener together so it makes one piece of fabric. Topstitch the seams either side of the hook-and-loop fastener, on the right side of the fabric.

6. Join the hook-and-loop fastener strip to the appliqué strip to make a continuous circle. Divide the fabric circle into four quarters and mark with pins (Fig. 2).

4. Cut the shorter, wider strip in half along its length to give you two strips. On one strip, press a 1.3cm (½in) seam allowance along one edge, wrong side to wrong side. On the other strip, press a 1.3cm (½in) seam allowance along one edge, right side to right side. Place the hook-and-loop fastener tape in the middle of each pressed seam allowance, so that it is 10cm (4in) in from each end, covering the raw edges (Fig. 1). Sew in place.

Fig. 2

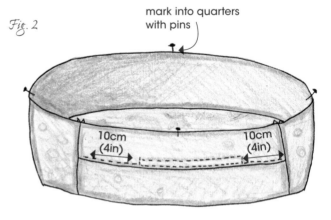

mark into quarters with pins

10cm (4in)   10cm (4in)

Fig. 1

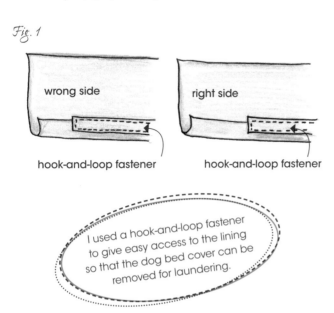

wrong side

right side

hook-and-loop fastener

hook-and-loop fastener

I used a hook-and-loop fastener to give easy access to the lining so that the dog bed cover can be removed for laundering.

Assemble and finish the bed

1. Attach the top rectangle to the side circle right sides together, matching up the pins. Pin each quarter well and ease excess fabric in. The accuracy of the insertion will depend on your seam allowances, pinning and fabric thickness, and nips and tucks may be necessary. Machine stitch. Remove pins. Zigzag stitch to finish all seams to prevent fraying.

2. Attach the bottom rectangle in the same way, and finish all seams as before.

3. Make the inner bag to the same dimensions as the bed, omitting the ric-rac and hook-and-loop fastener; leave a 15.5cm (6in) gap in one seam to fill with beans before closing up.

4. Turn the bed the right way out and insert the filled inner bag.

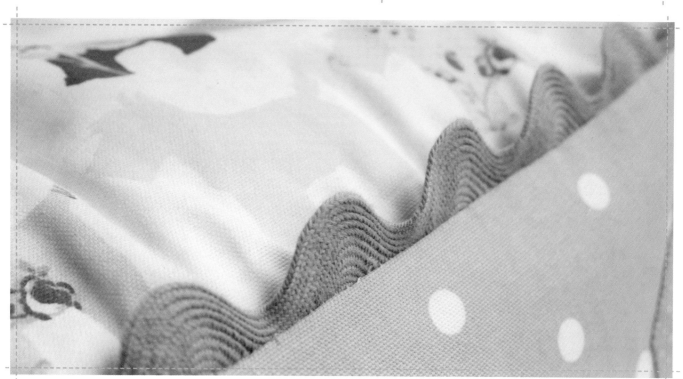

Dog Neckerchief

Pet accessories are all the rage at the moment and stores are even selling clothes to adorn your pets. I am not going that far with my beloved Ted, but a nice little scarf attached to his collar would make any dog look a dash cuter.

You will need
🏠 43.5cm x 30.5cm (17in x12in) cotton fabric

Finished size: 25.5cm x 15.5cm (10in x 6in)

Make the neckerchief

1. Fold the cotton fabric in half and half again, right sides together.

2. Enlarge the neckerchief pattern (see Patterns) and place on the folded fabric as marked. Cut out.

3. Open out the first fold and you will have the shape of the neckerchief in front of you, which includes a lining. Sew along the unfolded edges with a 6mm (¼in) seam allowance, leaving a 7.5cm (3in) opening in one side for turning. Trim the corners and turn the right way out. Press.

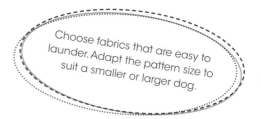

Choose fabrics that are easy to launder. Adapt the pattern size to suit a smaller or larger dog.

4. To make the casing for the dog's collar, turn over 3.2cm (1¼in) along the top edge and topstitch in place. Thread the collar through the casing, and it is ready to put on your dog (Fig. 1).

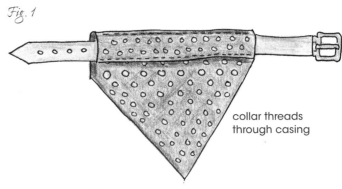

Fig. 1

collar threads through casing

Scruff Soft Toy

My own dog Ted has inspired the design of Scruff, a lovely soft toy made from fleecy fur, which makes him very appealing for children – big and small.

You will need

- 46cm (18in) square soft fleece fur
- Polyester stuffing
- Black embroidery thread
- Scrap of cotton fabric for scarf

Finished size: approx. 23cm x 18cm (9in x 7in)

Cut the pattern pieces and sew together

note: sew 6mm (¼in) seam allowances throughout.

1. Enlarge the patterns supplied (see Patterns) and use to cut the following pieces from the fleece fur: body x 2, ear x 4, head gusset x 1, leg gusset x 1 (note, the leg gusset should be cut on the fold).

2. Place the two body pieces right sides together and pin under the chin to the nose, A to B; sew.

3. Pin in the head gusset, B to C. Sew along one side from the nose to the back of the neck; then sew along the other side, stitching in the same direction. Continue to sew from C across the back and over the tail to D.

4. Pin in the leg gusset from A to D, and sew leaving a gap for stuffing in one side.

5. Gently stuff the dog and sew closed the opening with ladder stitch (see Techniques).

6. Place one set of ears right sides together; sew leaving the bottom edge open. Trim the seam and turn the right way out; oversew the bottom edge closed. Repeat for the other ear.

7. Pin the ears on top of the head, over the head gusset seam, and ladder stitch in place.

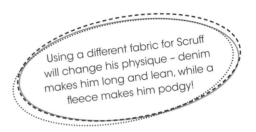

Using a different fabric for Scruff will change his physique – denim makes him long and lean, while a fleece makes him podgy!

Finishing off

1. Embroider French knots for Scruff's eyes and satin stitch his nose using all six strands of the embroidery thread.

2. Cut a small square of cotton fabric, fold in half diagonally, and tie around his neck.

Beach

Deckchairs are the quintessential icon of an English summer. They have made a big comeback and are now quite expensive to buy, but with a good rummage through second-hand shops and granny's garage you will find one you can lovingly restore. There is no better sight than a row of deckchairs lined up on a beach awaiting the holiday makers' arrival. My roomy beach bag will make sure you don't forget any essentials on your day out to the beach. And if you can't make it to the coast, string up a line of bunting in the garden, set up your deckchair beneath it, and dream of the sea.

Deckchair

Although any heavier weight upholstery fabric can be used to cover a deckchair, from summer roses to dramatic dots, I do love traditional stripes. I found a great company that specializes in deckchair canvas sold in exactly the right width in the most amazing colours (see Suppliers).

You will need

- 🏠 Deckchair
- 🏠 Sandpaper and sandpaper block
- 🏠 Wood stain and/or varnish
- 🏠 1.25m (48in) of 46cm (18in) deckchair canvas*
- 🏠 50cm (20in) square red dot fabric
- 🏠 Brown fabric offcuts
- 🏠 Fusible webbing
- 🏠 47cm (18½in) length of 1.3cm (½in) wide decorative tape
- 🏠 Tacks and hammer or staple gun

note: *this is a general rule of thumb and includes turnings, but if you are replacing an original covering, you should check the measurement once the old fabric is removed.

Prepare the deckchair

1. Remove the original seat fabric. Rub down the frame with sandpaper and stain and/or varnish to your desired finish.

2. Cut out the beach hut from red dot fabric (see Templates, Beach Hut Block and enlarge as required); use fusible webbing to attach it to the deckchair canvas, positioning it carefully so that the canvas stripe creates the door. Complete the door by working a line of stitching along the base of the hut. Make the roof by cutting two strips of brown fabric 1.3cm x 10cm (½in x 4in); fuse in place, overlapping onto the hut.

Prepare the seat bunting fringe

1. Use the medium bunting pattern (see Patterns) to cut out eight flags from red dot fabric.

2. Place the flags in pairs, right sides together, and stitch with a 6mm (¼in) seam. Trim the seam 2mm (³⁄₃₂in) from the stitching line; turn the right way out and press.

3. Topstitch each flag 4mm (⁵⁄₃₂in) around the edge by hand or machine.

Cover and finish the deckchair

1. Place one end of the prepared fabric, wrong side down, to the top front bar of the deckchair and fix in place by nailing tacks in 5cm (2in) apart across the top rail. (Alternatively, you can use a heavy duty stapler to staple it in place.)

2. Wrap the canvas around the top bar and bring it down to the bottom bar, opening out the chair so the canvas is very loose. Wrap it around the bottom bar and tack or staple in place (this is not quite so easy to do and you may need a friend to assist you).

3. Tack (or staple) the bunting flags to the front edge of the bottom rail, covering up the raw edges with the decorative tape, tucking in 6mm (¼in) at each end. Now find the sun!

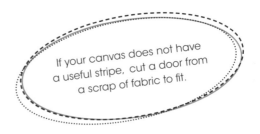

If your canvas does not have a useful stripe, cut a door from a scrap of fabric to fit.

Beach Bag

On childhood days spent at the beach, my mother's bag was always miraculously full of exactly what we'd need – towels, buckets and spades, a spare fleece for when the wind got up, a newspaper – and a pen for doing the crossword – as well as a flask and plenty of snacks. The best beach bags are big and beautiful!

You will need

- 70cm x 93cm (27½in x 36½in) blue fabric for the main bag*
- 1.2m (47in) of 106cm (42in) wide red large dot fabric for lining of bag, pocket and inside base
- 70cm x 47cm (27½in x 18½in) oilcloth for base/pocket**
- 56cm x 81cm (22in x 32in) cotton fabric for bag handles***
- Fabric offcuts for bunting flags and beach hut appliqués
- 7.5cm x 5cm (3in x 2in) white felt
- 96.5cm x 106cm (38in x 42in) thin cotton wadding for bag and handles
- 25cm (10in) fusible webbing
- 89cm (35in) each of narrow and medium ric-rac
- 140cm (55in) extra wide ric-rac
- Embroidery threads to match
- Two large and three small buttons
- 52cm x 30.5cm (20½in x 12in) medium-weight iron-on interfacing
- 15.5cm (6in) elastic
- 15.5cm x 50cm (6in x 20in) plastic canvas****
- Two 50cm (20in) wooden dowels
- 50cm (20in) decorative tape or ribbon
- Lobster claw clip
- Two magnetic clasps

Finished size: 68.5cm x 56cm (27in x 22in)

note: * light upholstery weight but nothing too thick as the wadding and lining will add weight to the bag; ** an oilcloth fabric is used to make the bag waterproof; if you prefer you can use ordinary fabric but be warned, your snacks may get soggy (for tips on working with oilcloth fabric, see Get Ready to Stitch); *** I have used the same dark pink large dot fabric used for the lining, but any coordinating fabric is fine; **** this gives support to the bottom of the bag, although you could use very thick card instead.

Prepare the base/pocket

1. Cut a piece of lining fabric 70cm x 47cm (27½in x 18½in). Cut two pieces of extra wide ric-rac 70cm (27½in) long.

2. Take the oilcloth fabric and place the ric-rac along the long edges with the humps of the ric-rac overlapping the edge, so that when you sew down the middle of the ric-rac you will have a 1.3cm (½in) seam. Sew in place with a large machine stitch.

3. Place the lining and the oilcloth fabric right sides together, and stitch together following the ric-rac line. Trim the seam and turn the right way out (Fig. 1). Press with your fingers.

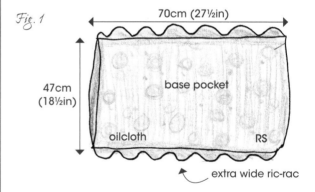

Fig. 1

70cm (27½in)

47cm (18½in)

base pocket

oilcloth

RS

extra wide ric-rac

4. If your machine has a walking foot attachment, you can topstitch along the edge to hold the ric-rac in place. If not, the magnetic clasp that you put on later will help to keep the layers flat.

Appliqué and decorate the bag fronts

1. Mark a line 24cm (9½in) in from the top and bottom edges of the main fabric.

2. Using the fusible webbing, the fabric offcuts and the beach hut template (see Templates, Beach Hut Block), appliqué three beach huts – two large and one small – to stand in a line on the top marked line (see Get Ready to Stitch). Cut strips of fabric for the roofs approx. 1.3cm x 10cm (½in x 4in) and fuse in place. Vary the size of the huts/roofs as I have done to create a less uniform effect.

3. Using a pencil, draw a wavy line above the beach huts and appliqué 12 bunting flags spread out along it. To complete the bunting, pin the narrow ric-rac along the marked line, and use a contrasting embroidery thread to sew the ric-rac in place by hand (Fig. 2). Finally appliqué the seagull using the white felt (use the seagull template from the Beach Hut Block and enlarge by 200%).

Fig. 2

4. Now turn the fabric around to decorate the opposite side of the bag front. Using the small bunting pattern (see Patterns), cut 14 flags from assorted red fabric offcuts. Place the flags in pairs, right sides together, and stitch with a 6mm (¼in) seam. Trim the seam 2mm (³⁄₃₂in) from the stitching line; turn the right way out and press. Topstitch each flag 4mm (⁵⁄₃₂in) from the edge by hand or machine.

5. Draw a wavy line 7.5cm (3in) down from the top edge. Place the flags on this line with an equal gap in between and sew in place. Pin the medium ric-rac on top of the edge of the flags and machine stitch down the middle of the ric-rac.

6. Cut a piece of wadding 70cm x 93cm (27½in x 36½in), spray lightly with spray adhesive and attach to the wrong side of the main fabric.

7. Quilt the beach huts and small bunting. Use a chunky running stitch and coton à broder. Backstitch the numbers 1, 2, 3 above the doors and sew on small button handles. Working on the opposite side of the bag, decorate the ric-rac braids using a contrasting thread as in Fig. 2.

Make the pockets and the lining

1. Place the base/pocket in the middle of the bag and pin in place along the extra wide ric-rac. (Do not pin along the oilcloth fabric as you will leave holes.) Machine-stitch through all layers to divide the base/pocket into segments, first from side to side, then from top to bottom (Fig. 3).

Fig. 3

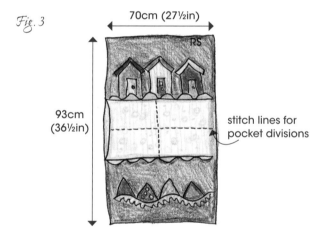

70cm (27½in)

RS

93cm (36½in)

stitch lines for pocket divisions

2. Fold the bag in half right sides together, and sew up the sides with a 1.3cm (½in) seam allowance. 'Sugar bag' the bottom corners of the bag (see Techniques). Trim the corner points and turn through.

3. Cut a piece of lining fabric 70cm x 93cm (27½in x 36½in). Fold in half wrong sides together, and sew up the sides with a 1.3cm (½in) seam allowance. 'Sugar bag' the lining but leave a 7.5cm (3in) opening in one side, and do not turn the right way through yet.

Make and attach the bag handles

1. From the handle fabric, cut four pieces each measuring 56cm x 20cm (22in x 8in). Cut two 56cm x 20cm (22in x 8in) pieces of thin cotton wadding.

2. From the interfacing, cut two pieces 52cm x 15.5cm (20½in x 6in). Cut the 'U' shape (see Patterns) from the middle of one long edge of the interfacing pieces.

3. Place two pieces of the handle fabric right sides together, and place on top of a piece of wadding. Lay the interfacing on top (Fig. 4). Pin well. Sew around the outside edge of the interfacing, through all layers, and leaving the bottom edge open. Trim the seams to 6mm (¼in), cut off the corners and snip the inside curve. Turn the right way out – use a teaspoon to smooth the curves and ease the corners.

Fig. 4

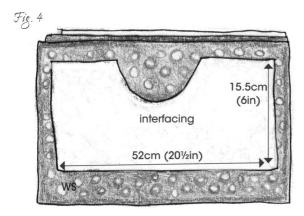

4. Topstitch all seams 6mm (¼in) in from the edge. Turn over 5cm (2in) to the wrong side to make the casing for the wooden dowel handles, and sew down (Fig. 5).

Fig. 5

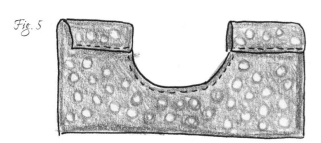

5. Repeat steps 3-4 to make a second handle. Place the handles to either side of the top of the bag right sides together, and pin really well. Sew using a large machine needle and go slowly as the layers are quite thick.

Assemble and finish the bag

1. Place the bag into the lining right sides facing and pin the top edges together. Sew. Turn the right way out through the gap left in the side of the lining. Press. Topstitch the seam, by hand if necessary using chunky running stitches.

2. Here is a clever little trick to prevent the sides of your bag from gaping. Cut two strips of coordinating fabric 4cm x 9cm (1½in x 3½in). Fold and press under a 6mm (¼in) hem on each side. Pin the strip 1.3cm (½in) down from the top of the side of the bag; stitch along the long sides through all layers to make a casing for the elastic. Thread the elastic into the casing and pin one end of the elastic beneath the folded side hem, and stitch over twice. Pull up the elastic until it measures approx. 5cm (2in); pin and sew as before. Trim off the elastic close to the stitching. Repeat on the other side of the bag.

3. To stabilize the base of the bag, make a casing to put the plastic canvas in. Cut a piece of fabric 32cm x 56cm (12½in x 22in) and fold in half. Sew one end and along one side, cut off the corners and turn the right way out. Slip the plastic canvas in and hand sew the open end closed. Secure in place at the bottom of the bag with a few stitches.

4. Thread the dowels into the handle casings and over sew at each end to close. Thread the lobster claw clip onto a 50cm (20in) length of decorative tape or ribbon and sew to the inside of the bag to keep your keys safe.

5. Finally attach the magnetic clasps to the inside and in the middle of the pocket on either side of the bag, following the manufacturer's instructions. Sew a large red button over the closure on the outside of the pocket.

Bunting

A day at the beach is incomplete without the sound of bunting flapping in the summer breeze. I have used a mixture of different fabrics including a nice red dot fabric to match the bunting trim on my deckchair, but you could just as easily use recycled fabric scraps.

You will need

- Plain and dot fabrics in several coordinating colours*
- 2m (2⅛yd) of 1.3cm (½in) ready-to-use bias binding tape

note: * in total 30.5cm x 107cm (12in x 42in) of fabric is required to make eight flags for a bunting length of 2m (2⅛yd).

Finished size: length 2m (2⅛yd); flag depth 13.5cm (5¼in)

Make the bunting flags

1. Using the large bunting pattern (see Patterns), cut out 16 flags from across your chosen fabrics.

2. Place the flags in pairs, right sides together, and stitch with a 6mm (¼in) seam. Trim the seam 2mm (³⁄₃₂in) from the stitching line; turn the right way out and press.

3. Topstitch each flag 4mm (⁵⁄₃₂in) from the edge by hand or machine.

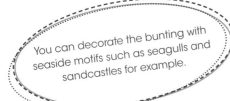

You can decorate the bunting with seaside motifs such as seagulls and sandcastles for example.

Finish the bunting

1. Attach the flags to the bias binding tape. Sew the first 25.5cm (10in) of the tape together to give you a good length for hanging.

2. Open out the fold of the bias binding tape, place a flag inside, pin and sew. Continue to sew the tape together for 5cm (2in) before opening out again to sew another flag inside.

3. Continue until all eight flags have been attached to the bias binding tape. Sew the remainder of the tape together for hanging.

Bunting is so easy to make – use fresh pinks, yellow and greens for a garden bunting and decorate with chickens, rabbits and flowers.

Village

As a child I was always making my dolls a house under a chair or in a box. My gran had a huge willow tree that we would play in, tying back the willows for curtains. When I had three daughters of my own, I designed (and my husband made) each a dolls' house – a sweet little cottage, a huge town house, and a shop with a flat above. This patchwork quilt, with its easy pieced block and simple appliqué shapes, gave me the chance to create a whole village. If you prefer, you can use individual appliqué blocks to make small wall hangings.

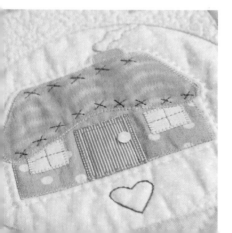

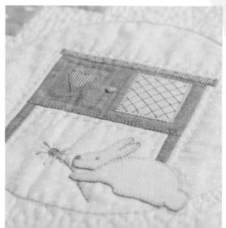

Patchwork Quilt

Before starting this project it is a good idea to review the essential information for working with fusible webbing and tips for machine appliqué outlined in Get Ready to Stitch. I have used machine blanket stitch for the appliqué worked with Maderia Lana in the needle. This is a wool mix thread that gives the illusion of hand appliqué.

You will need

Fabrics for the main quilt
- 76cm (30in) of 107cm (42in) wide pink large dot
- 115cm (45in) of 107cm (42in) wide cream small dot
- 61cm (24in) of 107cm (42in) wide blue stripe
- 50cm (20in) of 107cm (42in) wide blue dot
- 150cm (60in) of 150cm (60in) wide backing fabric

Fabrics for the appliqué
- 23cm (9in) square dark pink dot
- 10cm (4in) of 107cm (42in) wide pink stripe
- 23cm x 13cm (9in x 5in) blue stripe
- 23cm x 13cm (9in x 5in) blue small dot
- 23cm x 13cm (9in x 5in) blue wave
- 23cm x 18cm (9in x 7in) brown
- 23cm (9in) square light brown
- 23cm x 13cm (9in x 5in) pink floral
- 23cm x 13cm (9in x 5in) light brown dot
- Cream small dot fabric leftover from main quilt
- 10cm (4in) square cream felt
- 7.5cm x 5cm (3in x 2in) pink felt
- 7.5cm x 5cm (3in x 2in) cream calico

Pre-fused fabrics for the appliqué*
- 25.5cm x 13cm (10in x 5in) blue small dot
- 25.5cm (10in) square light brown
- 25.5cm x 13cm (10in x 5in) dark pink dot
- 25.5cm x 13cm (10in x 5in) cream small dot**
- 25.5cm x 13cm (10in x 5in) pink stripe
- 10cm x 2.5cm (4in x 1in) pink gingham
- 5cm (2in) square pink felt
- 13cm x 6.5cm (5in x 2½in) blue stripe

Other requirements
- 1m (39¼in) of fusible webbing
- 150cm x 150cm (60in x 60in) cotton wadding
- Machine threads to match fabric colours used
- Embroidery threads to match fabric colours used***
- 13 8mm pearl buttons for patchwork hearts
- Selection of small heart-shaped and pearl buttons for the appliqué

note: * it is easier and faster if you pre-fuse a selection of fabrics that will later be cut into rectangles, squares and strips for the appliqué decoration; ** for a different look, you can turn the cream small dot fabric over as I have done for the town house windows, for example; *** use either two strands of floss or one strand of coton à broder.

Finished size: 143.5cm x 143.5cm (56½in x 56½in)

Cut fabrics for the patchwork quilt

1. From the blue dot cut across the width of the fabric:
Two 11.5cm (4½in) strips;
Four 6.5cm (2½in) strips.

2. From the cream small dot fabric cut across the width of the fabric:
Two 11.5cm (4½in) strips;
Four 6.5cm (2½in) strips;
Three 21.5cm (8½in) strips cut into twelve 21.5cm (8½in) squares.

3. From the pink large dot cut across the width of the fabric:
Six 16.5cm (6½in) strips for the border.

4. From the blue stripe fabric cut:
Five 6.5cm (2½in) strips for sashing;
Five 6.5cm (2½in) strips for binding.

Make the patchwork blocks

1. Take two blue dot narrow strips and one cream small dot wide strip and sew them together with an accurate 6mm (¼in) seam allowance, so that the cream strip is in the middle. Press the seams to the centre. Repeat.

2. Carefully cut up the sewn strips into 26 sections each measuring 6.5cm (2½in). Note, you will have some fabric left over.

Fig. 1

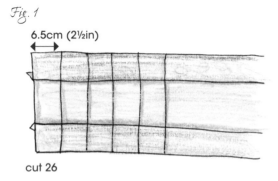

6.5cm (2½in)

cut 26

3. Take two narrow cream small dot strips and one wide blue dot strip and sew them together with an accurate 6mm (¼in) seam allowance, so that the blue strip is in the middle. Press the seams away from the centre. Repeat.

4. Carefully cut up the sewn strips into 13 sections each measuring 11.5cm (4½in). Note, you will have some fabric left over.

Fig. 2

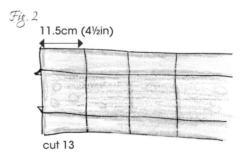

11.5cm (4½in)

cut 13

5. Sew two of the narrow pieced sections either side of a wide pieced section to make one complete patchwork block (Fig. 3). When joining sections, butt up the seam allowances (see Fig. 4); press. Make 13 blocks.

Fig. 3

Fig. 4

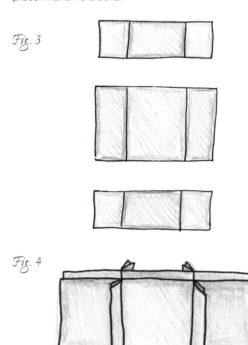

butting up seams

6. Appliqué a pink stripe heart into the centre of each block.

Notes for working the appliqué blocks

- 🏠 Each appliqué design is worked onto one of the 21.5cm (8½in) squares of cream small dot fabric.
- 🏠 Refer to the Templates for the pieces required to make each block.
- 🏠 The appliqué designs have been drawn in reverse where necessary.
- 🏠 Use the photograph of the block to guide you when positioning the fabric pieces for the appliqué.
- 🏠 All the appliqué is blanket stitched by machine unless otherwise specified.
- 🏠 I have used Madiera Lana thread (see Get Ready to Stitch for more details) in a 16/100 needle to give the appearance of hand stitching and an ordinary machine thread in the bobbin.
- 🏠 The quilting of the appliqué blocks is completed when the finished quilt is quilted.
- 🏠 All buttons are sewn on once the patchwork quilt has been completed to help to hold the layers together.

The caravan block

Appliqué Cut the caravan from the pink floral fabric and remove the door and windows – the fabric pieces cut for the door and windows are placed behind these openings. From pre-fused fabric, cut one blue small dot door 5cm x 7.5cm (2in x 3in) and two cream small dot windows 5cm x 4cm (2in x 1½in). Cut two blue stripe curtains and fuse on top of the windows before fusing behind the caravan. Add a cream window to the door. Cut two inner wheels from pink felt and fuse to two outer wheels cut from brown fabric. Fuse the finished wheels to overlap at the base of the caravan.

Embroider Backstitch the aerial in light brown.

Quilt Stitch around the outline of the caravan and the door, windows and wheels. Sew on a small heart button for the door handle.

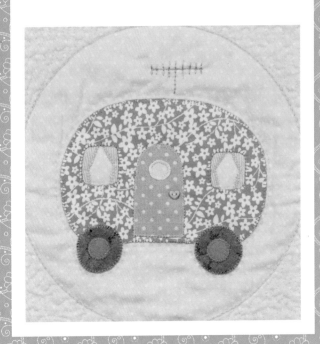

Make the beach hut block

Appliqué Cut the beach hut from blue stripe fabric, the sandcastle from light brown fabric, and four bunting flags from assorted pink fabrics; fuse in place. From pre-fused fabric cut a pink stripe door 4cm x 6.5cm (1½in x 2½in) and for the hut roof two strips of dark pink dot 7.5cm x 6mm (3in x ¼in). Cut the number 3 from dark pink fabric. Fuse these pieces on top of the hut. Cut the seagull from cream felt and fuse onto the roof apex.

Embroider Stitch tiny French knots for the seagull's beak and eyes. Backstitch the Union Jack in dark pink. Chain stitch the bunting string.

Quilt Stitch around the outline of the beach hut and sew on a small heart button for the door handle. To the sandcastle add a row of five tiny buttons and a star button above to represent shells.

The tree house block

Appliqué This design is created by layering the various parts to build up the image. Start by cutting the tree canopy from light brown dot fabric and fuse in place. Next cut the trunk and branches from brown fabric and fuse in position. Cut and fuse the tree house base using pink stripe fabric, the top and bottom edgings from blue small dot, and the roof from dark pink dot fabric. Cut two thin strips of pre-fused pink stripe fabric for the roof supports. Finally, add the bird which has been cut from cream felt.

Embroider Using brown thread, chain stitch the ladder so that it is propped against the base of the tree house; add the details to the bird – a French knot for the eye, satin stitch for the beak, and backstitch to define the wing's outline.

Quilt Stitch around the outline of the tree.

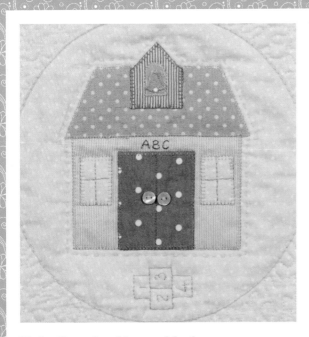

Make the school house block

Appliqué From pre-fused fabric, cut two cream small dot windows 2.5cm x 4cm (1in x 1½in), one blue stripe house 13cm x 6.5cm (5in x 2½in) and one dark pink dot door 5cm x 5.5cm (2in x 2¼in). Cut the roof from blue small dot. Appliqué these pieces in the following order: house, roof, windows, door. Now cut the bell tower from pink stripe and cut out the centre window, appliqué onto the roof and then add the bell cut from light brown fabric.

Embroider Using backstitch, add the ABC in pink above the school doors, the door division in pink, the window panes in light blue, and the hopscotch in taupe.

Quilt Stitch around the outline of the school house. Sew on two small buttons for the door handles.

Make the rabbit hutch block

Appliqué Cut from pre-fused fabric one light brown hutch body 10cm x 6.5cm (4in x 2½in) and two legs 4cm x 6mm (1½in x ¼in), a pink stripe top edging 11cm x 6mm (4¼in x ¼in), and a cream window 4.5cm x 4cm (1¾in x 1½in). Starting with the hutch body, fuse in place. Cut a pink stripe heart and fuse to the left of the window. Cut the rabbit from cream felt and fuse over the right leg of the hutch.

Embroider Chain stitch the flower stem (pink) and centre (brown); add lazy daisy petals in pink. For the rabbit, chain stitch a blue collar, satin stitch a black nose, and add a brown French knot eye. Backstitch the window grill in pink, and use brown thread to define the left-hand door of the hutch.

Quilt Stitch around the hutch outline and the rabbit. Sew on a pink heart button for the door handle.

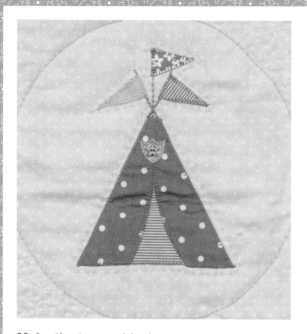

Make the teepee block

Appliqué Cut the outside of the teepee from the dark pink dot and the inside of the teepee from the pink stripe. Fuse the inside of the teepee onto the outside of the teepee. Cut two flags, one from the pink floral and one from the pink stripe fabric, and cut one in reverse from the blue stripe fabric. Fuse the flags in place leaving enough room for the teepee poles to be embroidered on later. Cut the shield from blue small dot fabric and appliqué just above the flaps of the teepee.

Embroider Using a taupe thread, chain stitch the poles of the teepee.

Quilt Stitch around the outline of the teepee, including the flags. Sew a star button on the shield.

Make the corner shop block

Appliqué Cut a blue wave roof, and a dog and number 37 from the cream small dot. From pre-fused fabric cut one pink stripe fascia 13cm x 2.5cm (5in x 1in), one pink gingham strip 9cm x 2.5cm (3½in x 1in) for beneath the display window, one pink felt door 5cm x 4cm (2in x 1½in), and 6mm (¼in) wide brown strips, two 5cm (2in), one 7.5cm (3in) and one 9cm (3½in) for window and door frames. Appliqué the shop pieces in place, adding the cream calico for the display window, finishing with the fascia board number and the dog at the door.

Embroider Using one strand of brown thread, backstitch the window display and herringbone stitch the arch. Satin stitch the dog's nose and add a French knot eye; chain stitch a red collar.

Quilt Stitch around the shop outline and sew on a button door handle.

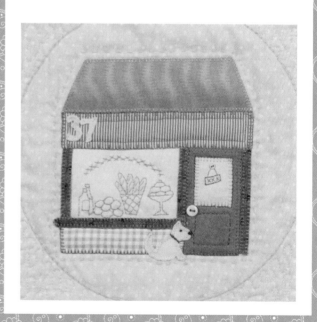

Make the town house block

Appliqué Cut the roof from blue small dot fabric and the chimney from brown fabric. From pre-fused fabric cut one brown house 9cm x 9.5cm (3½in x 3¾in), one dark pink dot door 5cm x 3cm (2in x 1⅛in), three cream windows 3.2cm (1¼in) square, six pink stripe curtains 6mm x 3.2cm (¼in x 1¼in), and two pink stripe strips 1.3cm x 7.5cm (½in x 3in) for the roof apex. Fuse the roof and house in place, laying the chimney beneath the roof. Now fuse the door and windows in position, and the roof apex. Finish by fusing the curtains to the windows.

Embroider Backstitch the sash windows in red.

Quilt Stitch around the outline of the house, the windows and the door. Sew on a heart button for the door handle.

Make the hen house block

Appliqué Cut the hen house from brown fabric. Cut the chicken body from blue wave fabric, the head from blue stripe and the comb from pink stripe. From pre-fused fabric cut two dark pink dot strips 6mm x 6.5cm (¼in x 2½in) for the roof, one light brown strip 6.5cm x 6mm (2½in x ¼in) for the hen house base, and two dark pink strips 4cm x 6mm (1½in x ¼in) for the hen house legs. Fuse and stitch in place. Cut a pink stripe door measuring 1.8cm x 2.5cm (¹¹⁄₁₆in x 1in) and a blue stripe heart (see the Rabbit Hutch Block) and fuse onto the hen house.

Embroider Using light brown, stitch the chicken's eye (French knot), beak (satin stitch) and feet (backstitch).

Quilt Stitch around the outline of the hen house and quilt the sunburst pattern above the chicken. Sew a star button on the heart.

Make the garden shed block

Appliqué Cut the shed (use the beach hut template from the Beach Hut Block) and the flowerpots from brown fabric. Cut a bird from cream felt (see the Tree House Block). Cut a piece of pink floral fabric measuring 4cm x 6.5cm (1½in x 2½in) for the door. From pre-fused fabric cut one cream window 2.5cm (1in) square and two strips of blue dot 7.5cm x 6mm (3in x ¼in) for the shed roof. Fuse and stitch in place overlaying the flowerpots on top of the shed at its base.

Embroider Chain stitch the bean pole canes in brown, and backstitch the window panes in blue. Work French knots for the beak and the eye of the bird, and backstitch the wing, all with brown thread.

Quilt Stitch around the outline of the shed, the door and the window. Sew on a heart button door handle and six star buttons for the flowers in the pots.

Make the rose cottage block

Appliqué Cut a piece of light brown dot fabric for the house measuring 13cm x 6.5cm (5in x 2½in). From pre-fused fabric cut one pink stripe door 4cm x 5cm (1½in x 2in) and two cream windows 2.5cm x 1.8cm (1in x ¾in). Place the house in place, and appliqué the windows and door on top. Cut a chimney from light brown fabric and a roof from wave fabric and appliqué in place, so that the chimney is behind the roof and the roof overlaps the house.

Embroider Using brown thread, backstitch the window panes in brown and work a smoke trail from the chimney. Using red thread, add a row of large cross stitches to the top and bottom edge of the roof, and chain stitch the heart motif beneath the house.

Quilt Stitch around the outside edge of the house. Sew on a pearl button for the door handle.

Make the dog kennel block

Appliqué Cut a kennel from dark pink spot, an inside kennel from light blue, a blanket from pink floral, the dog's head and body from brown fabric, and a bone from cream felt. Position the inside kennel and the blanket beneath the kennel and fuse in place. From pre-fused fabric cut two blue small dot strips 7.5cm x 6mm (3in x ¼in) for the roof and appliqué to the kennel. Appliqué the bone above the kennel door. When positioning the dog, place his head at a jaunty angle to give him a quizzical look.

Embroider Use brown thread to work the dog's legs in backstitch; add a French knot eye and satin stitch the nose.

Quilt Stitch around the outline of the kennel. Sew on the button for the dog's collar.

Join the patchwork and appliqué blocks

1. Join the blocks together in rows using Fig. 5 overleaf to guide you, and alternating patchwork blocks with appliqué blocks. For example, the first row starts with a patchwork block, then the caravan appliqué block, another patchwork block, then the tree house block, and finally another patchwork block. Sew the blocks together with a 6mm (¼in) seam and press open.

2. Press the seams of the sewn rows open and carefully join the rows together as in Fig. 5 overleaf. It is perfectly normal for some blocks not to be absolutely accurate, but a 6mm (¼in) out at the beginning of a row will mean 2.5cm (1in) out by the end of the row, so careful matching of the seams is important. Pin the seams that match and pull and ease the others to get the best fit you can. Press.

Add the sashing and the borders

1. Check the width of your quilt – it should measure 103cm (40½in) wide. Cut two of the 6.5cm (2½in) blue stripe strips to the width. Pin to the top and bottom edges of the quilt, starting at each end of the quilt, then ease the rest in along the width. Use lots of pins vertical to the seam. Sew and press open the seams.

2. Cut the remaining blue stripe strips to measure 113cm (44½in) – it will be necessary to join strips – and attach to the sides of the quilt as described above. Press open the seams.

3. Sew on the 16.5cm (6½in) pink large dot borders following the instructions for the sashing above. The measurements for the borders are 113cm (44½in) top and bottom and 143.5cm (56½in) on the sides; you will need to join the fabric strips to make the correct length, making sure you press the joined seams well.

Fig. 5

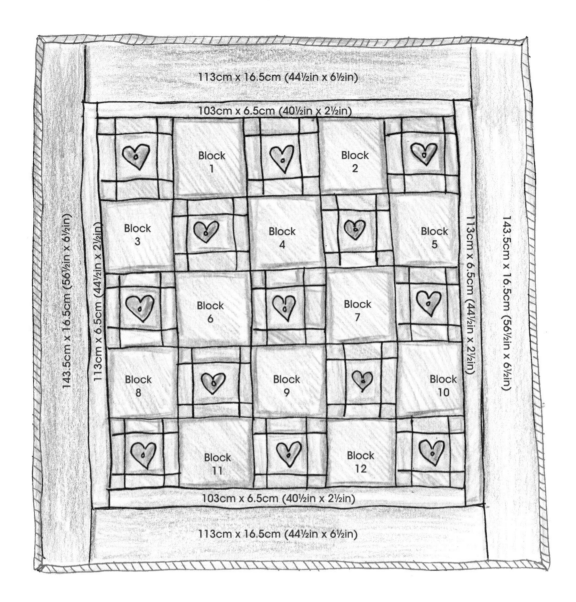

113cm x 16.5cm (44½in x 6½in)

103cm x 6.5cm (40½in x 2½in)

143.5cm x 16.5cm (56½in x 6½in)

113cm x 6.5cm (44½in x 2½in)

Block 1

Block 2

Block 3

Block 4

Block 5

Block 6

Block 7

Block 8

Block 9

Block 10

Block 11

Block 12

113cm x 6.5cm (44½in x 2½in)

143.5cm x 16.5cm (56½in x 6½in)

103cm x 6.5cm (40½in x 2½in)

113cm x 16.5cm (44½in x 6½in)

Key to appliqué blocks

Block 1 Caravan

Block 2 Tree House

Block 3 Beach Hut

Block 4 School House

Block 5 Rabbit Hutch

Block 6 Teepee

Block 7 Corner Shop

Block 8 Hen House

Block 9 Town House

Block 10 Garden Shed

Block 11 Rose Cottage

Block 12 Dog Kennel

Prepare for quilting

note: it is often said that 'quilting makes the quilt' and preparation is key to your success; do not be tempted to rush this part.

1. Carefully press all the seams and cut off any stray threads.

2. Cut a piece of backing fabric and a piece of cotton wadding at least 5cm (2in) bigger all around than the quilt top.

3. Lay the backing fabric on a flat surface wrong side facing you; smooth it out. Secure the fabric to the surface with a low-tack tape, ensuring that it is perfectly flat and under a little tension. Lay the wadding on top and smooth out flat. Place over the quilt top and smooth it out.

4. Pin the layers of the quilt together, using safety pins every 7.5cm (3in). Start in the middle and work your way out to the edges. Do not scrimp on pins as this will lead to rucks and creases. Once pinned, tack all the way around the edge of the border.

Quilt and embroider

note: I nearly always use a combination of machine and hand quilting on my quilts and the following describes how I quilted the patchwork quilt.

1. To stabilize the layered quilt, machine stitch-in-the-ditch around each block and along the borders, using an invisible or matching thread.

2. Use a 20cm (7¾in) diameter tea plate and a fine pencil to mark the circles on the appliqué blocks. Working with embroidery thread in a crewel embroidery needle, quilt using a chain stitch. Make sure your stitches go through to the wadding – they will look like a running stitch on the back.

3. Use an even, chunky running stitch to outline the hearts on the patchwork blocks as well as the parts of the designs previously described for each of the appliqué blocks.

4. I have intensively machine quilted the quilt with free-motion quilting around the outside of the appliqué block circles and in the border strips. This technique is not suitable for a beginner because it takes some practise to get the desired effect, but the quilt will look just as impressive without it.

5. Along the sashing strip I have hand-sewn a wavy row of chunky running stitches, working freehand. The stitches are neither perfect nor equal, but this gives the quilt a handmade look.

6. For the border, I again used free-motion quilting, but the less experienced may prefer to hand-quilt this. One idea is to take a house motif, make a cardboard template of it, and mark it randomly over the border, quilting with a chunky stitch. Six to seven houses at random angles across each border strip would look great.

7. Once the quilting is complete, sew on the decorative buttons and embellish with embroidery as described for each appliqué block.

My top quilting tips

- When I machine stitch-in-the-ditch I use YLI invisible thread as it never snags on the reel. It is available in smoke and clear, and a large reel lasts for ages.
- My favourite thread for hand quilting is DMC coton à broder. It is a single stranded thread, which is why I like it, and it is available in all colours – your sewing retailer will be able to order it for you.
- Madeira Lana, used for the machine appliqué for the patchwork quilt, is also suitable for quilting.
- Run your hand quilting thread through a beeswax candle to give it extra strength.
- To avoid unsightly knots when chunky stitching, put the needle in a couple of centimetres (an inch) away from the quilting start point and work a backstitch.

Bind the quilt

1. Cut the binding fabric into 6.5cm (2½in) wide strips and join to form one continuous length. Press open the seams. Fold in half lengthways and press.

2. Working with the right side of the quilt facing you, lay the binding along one side, matching the raw edges. Start 7.5cm (3in) from the beginning of the binding, and sew using a generous 6mm (¼in) seam.

3. Stitch until you reach one corner, stopping EXACTLY 6mm (¼in) from the end.

4. Pull the work away from the machine and fold the binding up so that it is aligned with the edge of the quilt, making sure it is straight.

5. Holding the corner, fold the binding back down, aligning it with the raw edge and making sure that the folded corner is square. Pin and sew over the fold continuing down the next side as in Fig. 6.

Fig. 6

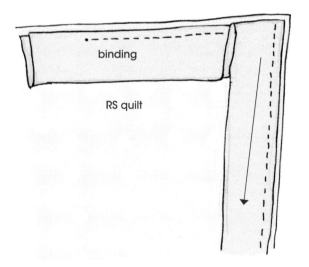

binding

RS quilt

6. Continue to bind around the quilt until you return to the starting point. Turn under 6mm (¼in) at the beginning of the binding. Place the end of the binding into the fold, trim to size and sew right over the top.

7. Fold the binding over to the back of the quilt and slip stitch in place. The corners will miraculously miter for you on their own.

8. Finally, don't forget to sign and date your completed quilt.

If you don't have time to make the patchwork quilt, choose your favourite motifs to design your own village scene to embellish the front of a cushion. This is a great way to use up fabric scraps and the cushion is quick and easy to make up (see Techniques for instructions on making an envelope back cushion). This would make a great house-warming gift.

Garden

I have always felt that the garden is an extension of the house, and when the weather is good we practically live outside, lounging on the deck with its lovely deckchairs, floor cushions and hanging baskets. On hot summer's afternoons, however, a tent can provide welcome shade for children, or even the family pet, and my easy-to-make and simple to erect teepee has been created with this in mind. I love to retreat to my garden shed with its special smell of good, warm earth. My seed packets are stored in the pockets of linen aprons hanging along the walls, and gardening books line the shelves. New additions to my collection of garden essentials are the coordinating garden kneeler and leaf collector.

Teepee

We have made our four children almost every traditional toy you can think of for birthdays and Christmas over the years, including dolls' houses, rocking horses, teddy bears and even a great tree house, but never a teepee. If only I had known it would be so easy!

You will need

- 🏠 3m (3¼yd) of 150cm (60in) wide main fabric with a non directional print*
- 🏠 2.5m (2¾yd) extra wide ric-rac
- 🏠 1.2m (47in) of 107cm (42in) wide contrasting fabric for the casing and appliqué
- 🏠 20cm (8in) square fusible webbing
- 🏠 5.5m (6yd) of 5cm (2in) wide binding tape
- 🏠 Four brass 'D' rings
- 🏠 Four 1.5m (60in) poles**
- 🏠 25.5cm (10in) adhesive hook-and-loop fastener
- 🏠 30.5cm (12in) sew-in hook-and-loop fastener

note: * this can be upholstery weight, denim or ordinary cotton, but the extra width is essential; ** bamboo or wooden dowels are also suitable. Use a 1.3cm (½in) seam allowance unless otherwise specified.

Finished size: 1.5m (60in) high x 1.2m (48in) square base

Cut the fabric

1. Fold the main fabric in half and cut to give you two 1.5m (60in) lengths. Take one piece and fold over 60cm (24in) of the width (Fig. 1). Cut off the unfolded section, and cut this strip in half along its length; put to one side to be used for facings later.

2. Returning to the folded piece of fabric, draw a straight line from the bottom left-hand to the top right-hand corner,

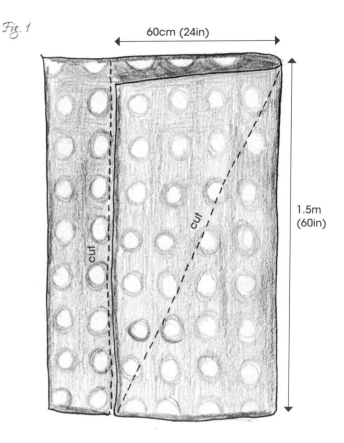

Fig. 1

60cm (24in)

cut

cut

1.5m (60in)

using a long stick or broom handle to help you. Cut along the diagonal line as shown in Fig. 1. This will give you one large triangle (side piece), and two half triangles, which will be joined to form the back. Pin the two triangles right sides together along the straight edge

3. Cut the remaining 1.5m (60in) of fabric in the same way but this time cut a rectangle 40cm x 30.5cm (15⅝in x 12in) from the cut strip (for the appliqué panel), and once the fabric is cut along the diagonal, do not pin the two half triangles together (these are the front flaps).

4. Cut three lengths from the extra wide ric-rac, two measuring 110cm (43⅛in) and one 30.5cm (12in).

5. Cut six 15.5cm (6in) strips from the contrasting fabric.

Make the teepee front

1. Sew together the two pinned half triangles; zigzag stitch to finish the seam to prevent it from fraying, and press.

2. Attach the long pieces of ric-rac to the right side of the straight edges of the remaining two half triangles, working from the wide bottom upwards (note, the ric-rac does not go all the way up to the top). Place the ric-rac with the humps overlapping the edge, so that when you sew down the middle of the ric-rac you will have a 1.3cm (½in) seam. Pin and tack (baste) in place, either by hand or with a large machine stitch.

3. To make a facing for each front flap, place a 30.5cm (12in) fabric strip right sides to the ric-rac, matching up the raw fabric edges, and pin in place. Sew on along the ric-rac tacking line. Trim off the ric-rac humps, turn the facing to the back of the front flap and press.

4. Fold half the facing back on itself and machine stitch in place. To give a nice firm edge to the front opening, topstitch 6mm (¼in) away from the ric-rac.

5. Lay out the two faced fronts with the ric-rac slightly overlapping so that the narrow ends are at the top. Place the appliqué panel rectangle at the top and pin in place; trim to match the triangle shape of the top of the teepee. Unpin the triangle and place the remaining ric-rac to the right side of the edge, with the humps of the ric-rac overlapping the edge, so that when you sew down the middle of the ric-rac you will have a 1.3cm (½in) seam. Once stitched, turn the seam to the wrong side and press. On the right side, you should now have only half of the humps of the ric-rac showing. Trim away the excess fabric from behind.

6. Cut a shield (see Templates) from contrasting fabric and use the fusible webbing to appliqué it to the top of the front of the tepee, using hand or machine blanket stitch to secure in place. If you wish you can embroider your child's name or initial onto the shield in backstitch.

Make the pole casings and assemble

1. Cut two of the contrasting fabric strips in half. Join a half strip to the end of the four remaining strips to make four 160cm (63in) lengths.

2. Fold under 6mm (¼in) at each end of the strips; press and sew in place. Fold all strips in half, right sides together, along their length. Sew one short end of the four casing strips closed and turn through.

3. Take one of the front pieces and, with its right side facing you, place one of the folded casing strips along the right-hand edge, so that the sewn up end is 2.5cm (1in) up from the bottom edge; match up the raw fabric edges and pin in place. Place a side piece (a whole triangle) on top, right sides together; re-pin and sew together.

4. Repeat to join the other front/side piece, and then again to join the two side/back seams. Zigzag stitch to finish all seams to prevent fraying.

Bind the teepee and make the peg loops

1. Fold the binding tape nearly in half and press really well. Starting at the front, pin the binding on the bottom raw edge of the teepee so that the shorter side is on top and the longer side folds around to the back – this will ensure you catch the binding on the wrong side of the fabric when you machine stitch it on.

2. To make the tent peg loops, cut four 5cm (2in) lengths of binding tape. To each, thread on a 'D' ring, fold in half and sew in place at each corner. Fold the remaining 50cm (20in) of binding tape in half, and pin the folded end to the top front edge of the teepee to protrude by 2.5cm (1in).

3. Turn the teepee inside out and sew across the top a couple of times to secure the tape in place, so that you can be sure it will firmly hold the poles in place once they are inserted into the casings.

Raise the teepee and fly the flags

1. Measure 1m (39¼in) up from the base of each pole and wrap a 5cm (2in) piece of the male (hook) part of the adhesive hook-and-loop fastener around it.

2. Thread the poles into the pole casings, pushing them down right to the bottom; gather the poles up at the top. Wrap the full length of the female (loop) part of the adhesive hook-and-loop fastener tape around the poles to secure them in position. Wrap the sew-in hook-and-loop fastener tape around the poles and secure in place above the adhesive hook-and-loop fastener tape. (You could tie a long scrap of fabric to cover the hook-and-loop fastener tapes.)

3. To make flags to fly from the pole ends, cut long thin triangles from the remaining fabric scraps approx. 35.5cm x 15.5cm (14in x 6in). Fold over the short straight edge by 5cm (2in) to make a pole casing, fold under a 6mm (¼in) hem and sew down the seam and across the top. To prevent fraying, zigzag stitch to finish the remaining raw edges.

Fig. 2

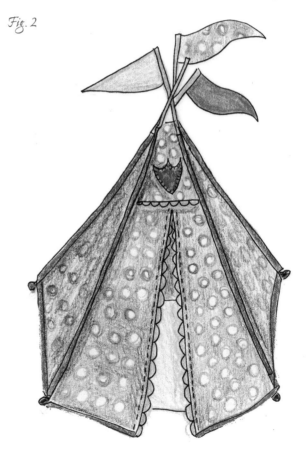

Garden Kneeler

Made from weatherproof oilcloth, this is invaluable for keen gardeners like me. As my back is not what it used to be, the garden kneeler is essential for weeding.

You will need

- 🏠 32cm x 94cm (12½in x 37in) oilcloth
- 🏠 96cm (37½in) of 5cm (2in) wide webbing tape
- 🏠 13cm x 15.5cm (5in x 6in) pink gingham
- 🏠 Fabric offcuts for the appliqué
- 🏠 18cm (7in) square fusible webbing
- 🏠 47cm x 32cm (18½in x 12½in) foam pad*

note: * foam pads sold as chair cushions can be cut to size very easily.

Finished size: 40.5cm x 25.5cm (16in x 10in) excluding handle

Make the kneeler

1. Cut two pieces of oilcloth measuring 47cm x 32cm (18½in x 12½in). Cut the webbing tape into three pieces each measuring 32cm (12½in).

2. Working on the right side of one of the oilcloth rectangles, sew a length of webbing tape to one of the short sides, overlapping 1.3cm (½in) from the edge. Zigzag stitch the cut edges of the tape to prevent them from fraying. Repeat for the second piece of oilcloth.

3. Cut the garden shed from the pink gingham fabric (see Templates, Beach Hut Block). Cut a 5cm x 9cm (2in x 3½in) rectangle of fabric for the shed door (I used a blue chenille fabric to replicate painted timber), a 4cm x 2.5cm (1½in x 1in) rectangle of fabric for the window, and two fabric strips approx. 2.5cm x 13cm (1in x 5in) for the roof. Cut a pot shape from a 2.5cm (1in) brown fabric square.

4. Appliqué the garden shed design in the centre of one piece of the oilcloth. When ironing on the fabrics with fusible webbing, protect the oilcloth with a tea towel (it is best to do a test piece first as some oilcloths are more sensitive than others to the heat of the iron). Sew the appliqué with a machine blanket stitch or zigzag stitch, as it is not easy to sew by hand.

5. To make the handle, fold the remaining length of webbing tape in half lengthways and sew along the long edge. Working on the appliquéd piece of the oilcloth, pin the handle to the wrong side of the webbing tape edging, approximately 7.5cm (3in) from each side. Sew in place.

6. Place both pieces of the oilcloth right sides together and sew around the sides and the bottom edge with a 6mm (¼in) seam allowance, leaving the top edge open.

7. 'Sugar bag' the bottom by squashing the side seams onto the bottom (see Techniques). Measure 2.5cm (1in) in from each point and sew a straight line across. Cut off the points and turn the right way out.

8. Fold the foam in half along its length and place inside the kneeler. (Folding the foam in half makes it easier to get it into the kneeler as it is a bit sticky; it will spring out to its full length once inside.) Sew along the top edge of the webbing tapes to finish. This may be difficult to stitch on the machine, so it is best to do it by hand with double thread.

You could convert the garden kneeler to make a cushion for your garden bench.

Leaf Bag

This bag comes in handy to transport leaves to the compost bin. It is made from weatherproof oilcloth to coordinate perfectly with the garden kneeler.

You will need

- 76cm (30in) square oilcloth
- 76cm (30in) square pink gingham
- 224cm (88in) of 5cm (2in) wide webbing tape

Finished size: 76cm x 76cm (30in x 30in)

To make the leaf bag

1. Tack (baste) the pink gingham lining and oilcloth wrong sides together (alternatively use a light covering of spray adhesive). Measure 7.5cm (3in) across each corner and cut off.

2. Bind the corners of the fabric with webbing tape. First cut four 7.5cm (3in) lengths of the tape and fold not quite in half lenghways; press well. Fold a length of tape over each corner so that the shorter side is on top and the longer side underneath; working from the top side, sew in place, making sure you catch the webbing tape underneath as you go.

3. Use the remaining webbing tape to bind the edges of the leaf bag and simultaneously make the handles (Fig. 1). First, fold the tape not quite in half and press well. Starting halfway down one side, place the shorter side of the webbing tape on top and the longer side underneath, and sew until you reach the cut-off corner. To make a handle, continue to sew along the tape edges only for 25.5cm (10in); then open out the tape to rejoin it to the next side. Continue sewing until you reach the next corner and repeat.

4. Continue in this way until you reach your starting point. Overlap the ends of the webbing tape to join and zigzag over the seam to prevent fraying.

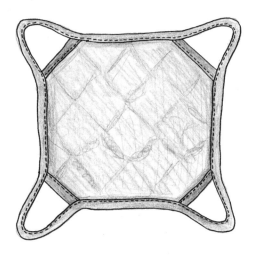

Fig. 1

With a different choice of fabrics, this project could convert to a toy bag – gather up those playthings and hang the bag on a hook.

House

These cushions were inspired by the art of paper cutting, and in particular by the talent of the English artist Rob Ryan, whose work I admire very much, and whose designs can now be found everywhere, decorating all sorts of objects including cards, ceramics and textiles. I thought the paper cutting technique could be used just as easily on felt and after a little playing around I came up with these super house designs. They are so fun and easy to make that before I knew it I had the beginnings of a town, with three large cushion designs and a fourth for a sweet little pin cushion.

Cutwork Cushions

I was inspired by the art of paper cutting when designing these cushions. They are so easy and fun to make and using felt for the cutwork technique is perfect as it doesn't fray. Once you have made one there will be no stopping you – luckily you have three to choose from!

You will need (for each cushion)

- 20cm (8in) square felt
- 20cm (8in) square fusible webbing
- Two 37cm (14½in) squares wool blanket
- Polyester stuffing
- One skein embroidery thread to match felt

Finished size: 35.5cm x 35.5cm (14in x 14in)

Make the cutwork panels

1. Trace your chosen house template (see Templates) onto fusible webbing. Add the penny border to the design (note, the template provided is only one quarter of the border, so you will have to turn and trace for the other three corners).

2. Fuse the design onto the wrong side of the felt square following the instructions for working with fusible webbing (see Get Ready to Stitch).

3. Cut out the shaded area of the design very neatly with small scissors. This may be quite a challenge depending on how thick your felt is, and sharp scissors are essential. The sharper the scissors, the neater the cut, the easier to blanket stitch later.

Fuse and sew felt panel to cushion front

1. Peel off the backing from the fusible webbing and position the cutwork felt panel in the centre of one of the wool blanket squares. Iron in place. If the fabric is thick, you may have to iron from both sides to get the fusible webbing hot enough to adhere; be careful not to scold the fabric. For the Rose Cottage design fuse the heart cut from the roof in the centre of the doorway.

2. Blanket stitch around all the cut edges of the design by hand or machine, using a thread colour that perfectly matches the felt.

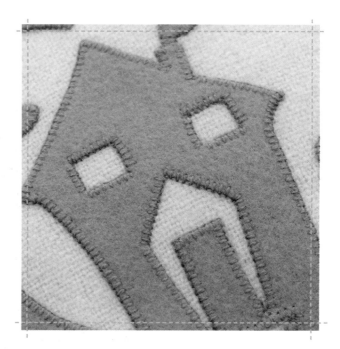

The blanket stitch detail was worked on the sewing machine using Maderia Lana (a wool-effect thread) in the needle and an ordinary sewing thread in the bobbin.

Finish the cushion

1. Pin the cushion front to the cushion back, right sides together. Sew around all four sides using a 6mm (¼in) seam allowance, leaving a 7.5cm (3in) opening in one side for stuffing. Trim across the fabric at each of the corners to ensure a neat finish, and turn the right way out.

2. Blanket stitch along the edges working big, chunky stitches approximately 1.3cm (½in) wide. DO NOT SEW OVER THE OPENING. Finally sew a running stitch 4cm (1½in) in from the edge, again leaving the opening unstitched.

3. Firmly stuff the cushion. To close the opening, continue the blanket stitch and running stitch detailing as in step 2.

4. To finish the Rose Cottage design, work a line of backstitches across the top of the picket fence.

Cutwork Pin Cushion

This little pin cushion is made in exactly the same way as the large cutwork cushion and it is an ideal project for those of you who have scraps of felt just begging to be used up.

You will need

- 🏠 13cm (5in) square teal felt
- 🏠 13cm (5in) square fusible webbing
- 🏠 Pink felt offcut
- 🏠 Two 15.5cm (6in) squares wool blanket
- 🏠 Wool fleece stuffing
- 🏠 One skein pink embroidery thread

Finished size: 15.5cm x 15.5cm (6in x 6in)

Make the pin cushion

1. Trace the cotton reel cottage template (see Templates) onto fusible webbing and fuse onto the wrong side of the felt square following the instructions for working with fusible webbing (see Get Ready to Stitch).

2. Cut out the shaded area of the design very neatly with small, sharp scissors.

3. Fuse the design into the middle of one of the wool blanket squares; cut a small heart from pink felt and fuse it in the middle of the cotton reel. Blanket stitch around the edges with one strand of coton à broder or two strands of stranded cotton (floss).

4. Place the two wool blanket squares wrong sides together and blanket stitch around the outside edge, leaving an opening for stuffing; sew a line of running stitches inside the blanket stitch.

5. Stuff; then finish off the running stitch and blanket stitch to close the opening.

If you use a natural wool fleece such as alpaca for stuffing, the natural oils of the fleece will prevent your needles from rusting.

Christmas

At Christmas time the children and I would almost always make a traditional gingerbread house held together with icing sugar and decorated with all sorts of sweets in quantity. It took some eating. Now that my children are older, I thought I would make a fabric version to remind them of the fun we had baking our own. Filled with gingerbread biscuits, this makes the perfect gift – that's if you can bear to give it away! Following on from this theme, I decided to make some delightful little gingerbread men to decorate the Christmas tree.

Gingerbread House

The best bit about making this little gingerbread house is the decorating. You could go really mad with all the lovely festive buttons and ribbons you can buy. However, I have chosen a more subtle snow-and-ice inspired cream ric-rac braid and pearl button heart motif.

You will need

- 🏠 46cm x 30.5cm (18in x 12in) thick interfacing
- 🏠 46cm x 30.5cm (18in x 12in) thin cotton wadding
- 🏠 50cm (20in) of 106cm (42in) wide brown cotton fabric
- 🏠 25.5cm (10in) square fusible webbing
- 🏠 Red small dot, pink stripe and cream fabric offcuts
- 🏠 132cm (52in) cream narrow ric-rac
- 🏠 40.5cm (16in) cream wide ric-rac
- 🏠 18cm x 20cm (7in x 8in) cream felt
- 🏠 One skein cream embroidery thread
- 🏠 Eight 1.3cm (½in) pearl buttons
- 🏠 35 6mm (¼in) pearl buttons
- 🏠 Wooden kebab stick
- 🏠 Drinking straw
- 🏠 Two wooden beads*

note: * choose beads to fit the end of the kebab stick.

Finished size: 15.5cm x 13cm x 15.5cm (6in x 5in x 6in) excluding chimney

Cut and prepare the house pieces

1. From the interfacing and cotton wadding, cut the following: one base 15.5cm x 13cm (6in x 5in); two sides 15.5cm x 7.5cm (6in x 3in); and two roofs 10cm x 18cm (4in x 7in). Using the gable end template (see Templates), also cut two gable ends.

2. Glue the wadding to the interfacing with a light spray of fabric adhesive. (Alternatively, tack the layers together at step 4 below.)

3. Fold the brown fabric in half. Lay the interfacing/wadding pieces on top, leaving a 5cm (2in) gap in between. Cut out the pieces 2.5cm (1in) bigger all around to give you two sets of brown fabrics pieces for each house part. Put one set aside.

4. Using spray fabric adhesive, glue the other set of brown fabric pieces to the wadding side of each house part, centring the pieces in the middle of the fabric. Alternatively, tack the layers together now.

Fast2Fuse – a thick, iron-on interfacing that is very easy to sew through – will save you time (see Suppliers).

Make the windows and doors

1. Draw one 5cm x 7.5cm (2in x 3in) rectangle and three 4cm (1½in) squares onto the smooth side of the fusible webbing, and cut out roughly.

2. Iron the rectangle onto the wrong side of the dot fabric for the door, and the squares onto the stripe fabric for the windows. Cut out neatly.

3. Peel off the paper and iron the door to one of the gable ends, and a window on the other. Fuse a window on each side of the house, placing them about 2.5cm (1in) up from the bottom edge. Blanket stitch the doors and windows by hand or machine.

Complete the fabric pieces

1. Place the set-aside brown fabric pieces right sides together with the other set of prepared house parts. Stitch together all the way around the edge of the interfacing, leaving a 5cm (2in) opening at the bottom for turning.

2. Trim off the excess brown fabric, cut across the corners and turn the right way out. Poke out the corners with the end of a spoon. Sew the opening closed. Gently press.

Add the gable end and side decoration

1. On the gable ends and sides of the house, tack (baste) the narrow ric-rac 6mm (¼in) in from the edge at the top and sides. Stitch in place through the middle of the ric-rac.

2. Cut two side snowlines and two gable end snowlines from cream felt (see Templates). Prepare with fusible webbing and appliqué the snowlines in place along the bottom edge with blanket stitch. Note, you will need to cut one gable end snowline in half to position on either side of the appliquéd door.

3. Cut two small hearts (see Templates) from cream felt and appliqué above the window and door at the gable ends. Cut a 2.5cm (1in) cream fabric window and appliqué to the door. Embroider a chain stitch border around the windows and doors. Blanket stitch the doors and windows by hand or machine.

4. Sew two 1.3cm (½in) buttons on either side of the windows and door. Add a 6mm (¼in) button for the door handle, and another to the centre of the small felt hearts.

Chain stitch emphasizes a shape and will make that area of the design look more prominent.

Add the roof decoration

1. Tack (baste) the wide ric-rac along the bottom edge of the two roof pieces, tucking under at each end. Sew in place.

2. Mark the large heart design with a fine pencil onto each roof piece. For each pearl button heart, sew on 16 of the small pearl buttons following the outline.

3. Cut one roof snowline from cream felt (see Templates). Prepare with fusible webbing and cut out the shaded area in the middle of the template (this slit will accommodate the chimney later).

4. Place the roof pieces together with a 1.3cm (½in) gap between the two. Centre the roof snowline over the gap and fuse in place. Blanket stitch around the snowline by hand, and sew to secure to the top inside edge of the roof.

5. For the chimney, cut two pieces of white felt 2.5cm x 7.5cm (1in x 3in); hand-sew together with blanket stitch down the long sides. Fold in half and sew the ends together to make a loop. Pop the sewn end through the roof slit from the right side (it will be secured later).

Build the house

1. At the apex of each gable end you need to make a loop to accommodate the wooden kebab stick which will hold up the roof. Sew four stitches on top of each other 6mm (¼in) wide to make a loop. Blanket stitch the loop by sewing over the stitches only and not picking up any of the fabric beneath.

2. Sew the bottom of the four side sections of the house to the base with a ladder stitch, using a doubled matching brown thread.

3. Match up the sides of the house and sew together using white thread when joining the snowlines and brown thread for the house.

4. Cut the wooden kebab stick to size 18cm (7in) long and thread through the first gable end loop and glue on a bead. Thread a 15.5cm (6in) length of drinking straw onto the stick (the straw will help to keep the gable ends from collapsing). Thread the straw-covered stick through the chimney loop, and the end of the stick through the loop at the other gable end; glue on the other bead to secure in place. Stitch the chimney in place from the right side. Your finished house is now ready to be filled with biscuits!

Tree Decorations

I am not a fan of themed trees – I prefer mine to be decorated with handmade hangings that are all a little bit different. It's so exciting getting the box down from the attic to find something I made last year but had completely forgotten about. This year I shall add these cheery little gingerbread men to my decorating stash.

You will need (to make one decoration)

- 13cm x 30.5cm (5in x 12in) brown fabric
- Handful of polyester stuffing
- Red embroidery thread
- Two black micro buttons
- Three small heart buttons
- Three round gingham buttons
- 13cm (5in) length of narrow gingham ribbon

Finished size: 10cm x 13cm (4in x 5in)

Make the gingerbread man

1. Trace off the gingerbread man pattern (see Patterns), stick onto card and cut out.

2. Fold the brown fabric in half right sides together and pin. Using a pencil, draw around the gingerbread man outline. DO NOT CUT OUT.

3. Stitch on the marked line with a small stitch, leaving an opening in one side. Cut out close to the stitch line and snip into either side of the neck, the armpits and the crotch.

4. Gently turn the gingerbread man the right way out. Stuff, then sew closed the opening.

5. Blanket stitch all around the outside edge with one strand of coton à broder or two strands of stranded cotton (floss).

Decorate the gingerbread man

1. Sew on two small black buttons (or beads) for his eyes, sewing through to the back to create an indentation.

2. Sew on the two small heart buttons for his cheeks and backstitch a smiling red mouth from button to button. Sew on the three gingham buttons down his chest.

3. Fold the gingham ribbon in half and secure it at the back of the head with the remaining heart-shaped button to make a hanging loop.

To make turning through the limbs easier, poke a drinking straw into the arm/leg, push a wood skewer into the end of the straw and roll the arm/leg onto the skewer.

Techniques

Step-by-step instructions are provided in the project chapters to enable you to make the beautiful things featured. But when you need a little more help, the more detailed advice in this section will clarify some key techniques.

Binding

Bindings decorate and finish a raw edge at the same time. The binding can be made using the project fabric as for the double-bound edge of the Union Jack Tea Cosy, or ready-made binding can be bought as for the Sewing Machine Cover.

For the Union Jack Tea Cosy, take the remaining 6cm (2½in) pink stripe fabric strip and fold 6mm (¼in) under at one end and press. Fold the binding in half along its length, wrong sides together, and press. Working on the right side of the cosy and starting at a seam, match the raw edge of the binding to the raw edge of the tea cosy and pin all the way around. Leaving the first 5cm (2in) of binding unsewn, stitch in place with a 1.3cm (½in) seam. When you get back to where you started, tuck the unfinished end into the unsewn binding, pin well and sew straight across. Press the binding to the inside of the tea cosy and slip stitch in place.

Ric-rac decoration on the Union Jack Tea Cosy.

For the Sewing Machine Cover a ready-made binding is used. Ready-made binding comes pre-folded, and once opened out it should have three creases. Open out the binding and place it right sides together with the bottom of the cover, raw edges matching. Start and finish at one side. Fold over the beginning of the binding by 6mm (¼in). Sew in the first crease of the binding. When you come to the end overlap onto the beginning of the binding and sew over both layers of binding. Fold the binding to the wrong side of the cover, so that the second crease of the binding becomes the bottom edge of the cover; tuck under the last crease of the binding and slip stitch in place.

Edging with ric-rac braid

I love ric-rac braid and often use it to edge my projects. It is available in different widths and the edging technique used differs slightly according to the ric-rac width used.

Edging with medium/wide ric-rac

It is important to position and machine the ric-rac carefully to prevent the humps of the ric-rac from disappearing when the project is turned the right way out. Working on the right side of the fabric, line up the edge of the ric-rac with the raw edge of the fabric. Tack (baste) in place by machine stitching down the middle of the ric-rac. When starting and finishing the edging keep the ends out of the way by tucking them back on themselves to leave the seam allowance ric-rac free (Fig. 1).

Fig. 1

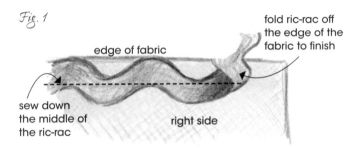

edge of fabric

fold ric-rac off the edge of the fabric to finish

sew down the middle of the ric-rac

right side

Edging with extra wide ric-rac

Working on the right side of the fabric, place the extra wide ric-rac so that it overlaps the raw edges of the fabric as shown in Fig. 2 and pin in place. Sew a line of machine stitching 6mm (¼in) from the fabric edge down the middle of the ric-rac braid. When starting and finishing the edging keep the ends out of the way by tucking them back on themselves to leave the seam allowance ric-rac free.

 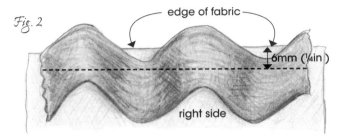

Fig. 2

edge of fabric

6mm (¼in)

right side

Sugar bagging

This technique is used to create a flat base to the Beach Bag and the Garden Kneeler. Once the side seams have been sewn and before turning through to the right side, squash the side seams onto the bottom (Fig. 3) to 'sugar bag' the bottom corners. For the Beach Bag measure 6cm (2½in) in from each point and sew a straight line across; for the Garden Kneeler measure just 2.5cm (1in) in. Once the straight line has been sewn, the points should be cut off.

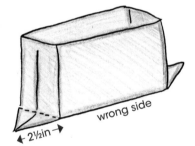

Fig. 3

wrong side

2½in

Making an envelope back cushion

To make a cushion with a finished size of 50cm x 30.5cm (20in x 12in), you will need 1.75m (70in) of wide ric-rac, 50cm (20in) of 107cm (42in) wide fabric, and 52.5cm x 33cm (21in x 13in) of cotton-mix wadding.

Cut a piece of fabric 51.3cm x 32cm (20½in x 12½in) for the cushion front. Decorate the right side of the fabric with the appliqué design of your choice and spray glue the wadding to the wrong side of the decorated fabric. Using one strand of coton à broder and a chunky running stitch, quilt around the outside edge of the appliqué design. Pin the ric-rac braid all the way around the cushion starting halfway down one side. To avoid creating ugly points at the corners, curve the ric-rac around each corner easing it round.

To make the cushion back, cut two pieces of fabric 13cm x 32cm (5in x 12½in) and 46cm x 32cm (18in x 12½in). Hem one 32cm (12½in) edge on each fabric piece. Overlap the two hemmed pieces of fabric to measure 51.3cm x 32cm (20½in x 12½in); pin together.

Pin the cushion back to the cushion front, right sides together, and sew around the outside edge sewing on the same line as the ric-rac. Cut off the corners and trim the seams. Zigzag stitch over the seams to prevent fraying, turn the right way out and insert a cushion pad.

Utility stitches

Perfect these hand finishing stitches for a professional finish to your projects.

Ladder stitch

For closing a seam on a stuffed item or sewing two folded edges together. The stitches look like a ladder until they are pulled tight to close the seam. Knot the end of the thread and start from inside the opening to hide the knot. Take straight stitches into the folded fabric, stitching into each edge in turn. After a few stitches pull the thread taut to draw up the stitches and close the gap.

Slip stitch

Also used to close gaps in seams. When worked neatly, it is almost invisible. Work from right to left, picking up a tiny piece of the fabric from one seam edge. Insert the needle into the other seam fold and move the needle along 3mm (⅛in). Push the needle out into the seam edge and repeat.

Templates

note: The appliqué patterns have been drawn in reverse where necessary and this has been indicated with (R).

Place Setting Tablecloth

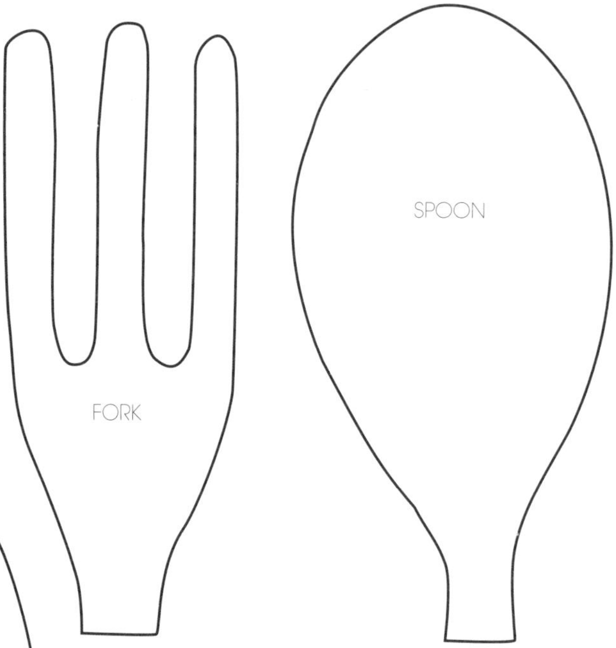

FORK

SPOON

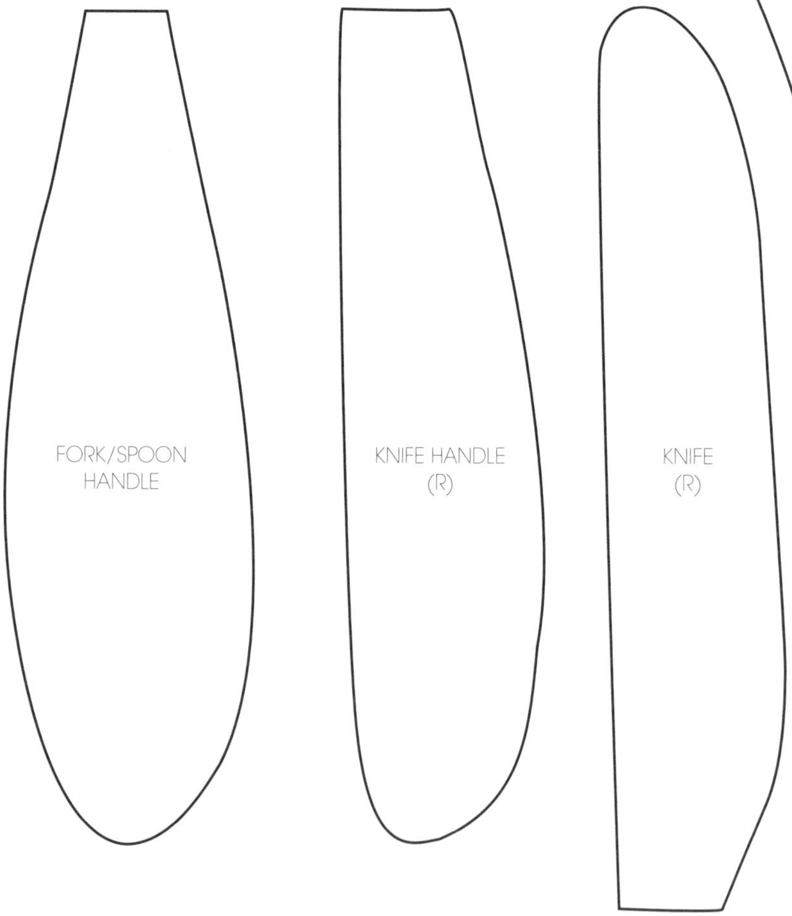

FORK/SPOON
HANDLE

KNIFE HANDLE
(R)

KNIFE
(R)

Dog Bed

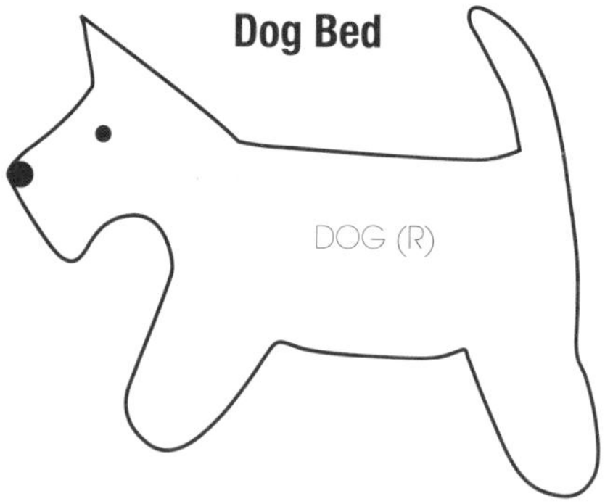

DOG (R)

Sampler Picture

Sewing Machine Cover

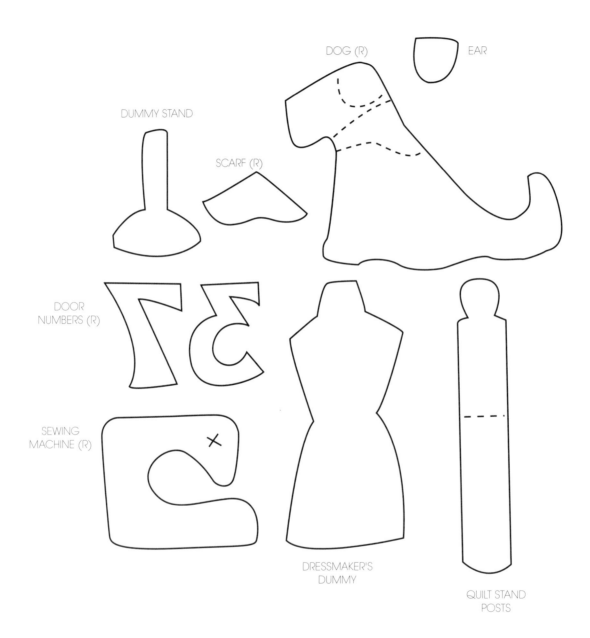

DOG (R)

EAR

DUMMY STAND

SCARF (R)

DOOR
NUMBERS (R)

SEWING
MACHINE (R)

DRESSMAKER'S
DUMMY

QUILT STAND
POSTS

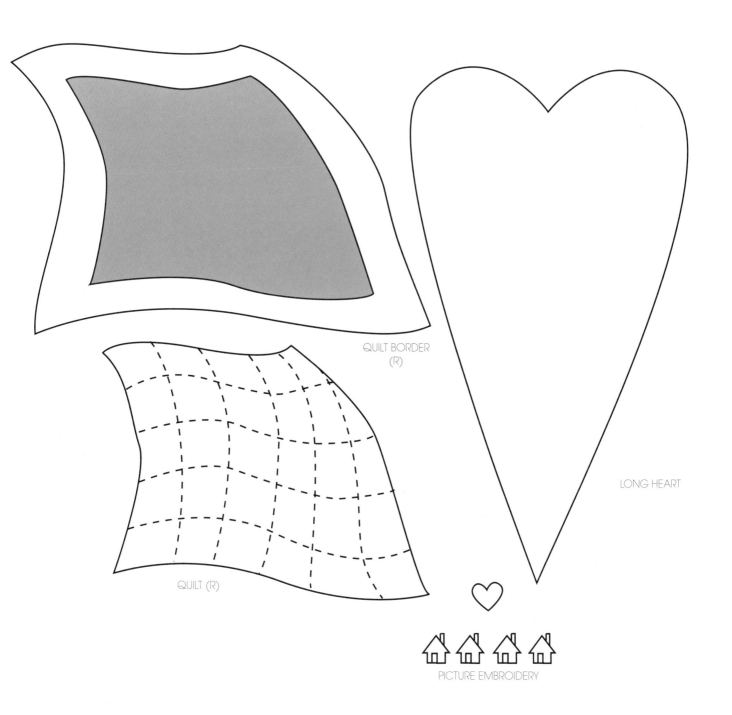

QUILT BORDER
(R)

QUILT (R)

LONG HEART

PICTURE EMBROIDERY

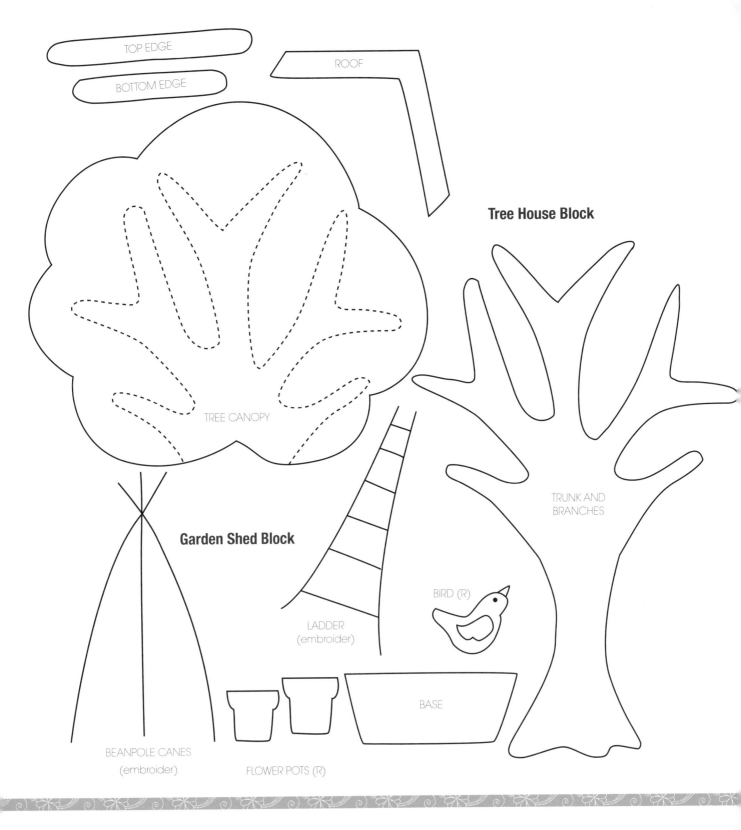

TOP EDGE

BOTTOM EDGE

ROOF

Tree House Block

TREE CANOPY

Garden Shed Block

TRUNK AND
BRANCHES

LADDER
(embroider)

BIRD (R)

BASE

BEANPOLE CANES
(embroider)

FLOWER POTS (R)

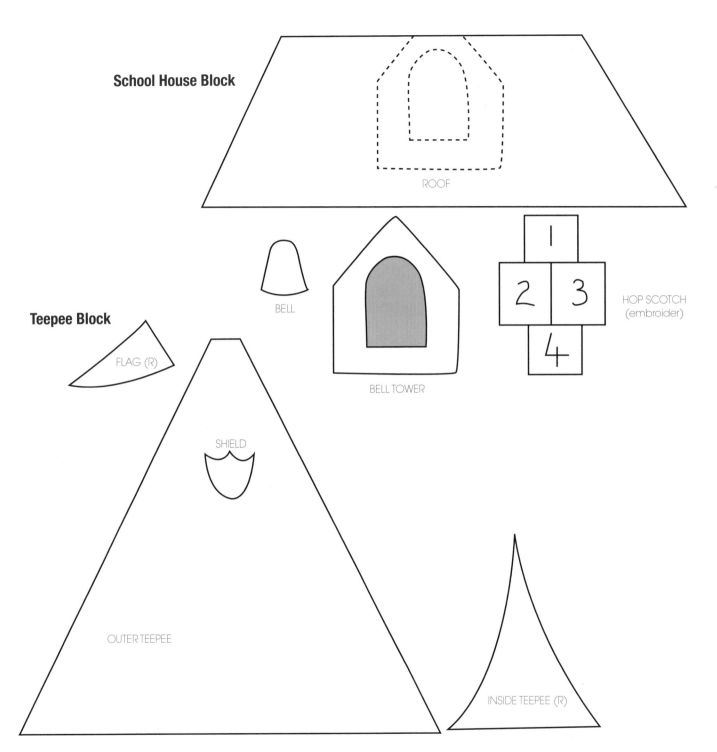

School House Block

ROOF

BELL

BELL TOWER

HOP SCOTCH
(embroider)

1

2 3

4

Teepee Block

FLAG (R)

SHIELD

OUTER TEEPEE

INSIDE TEEPEE (R)

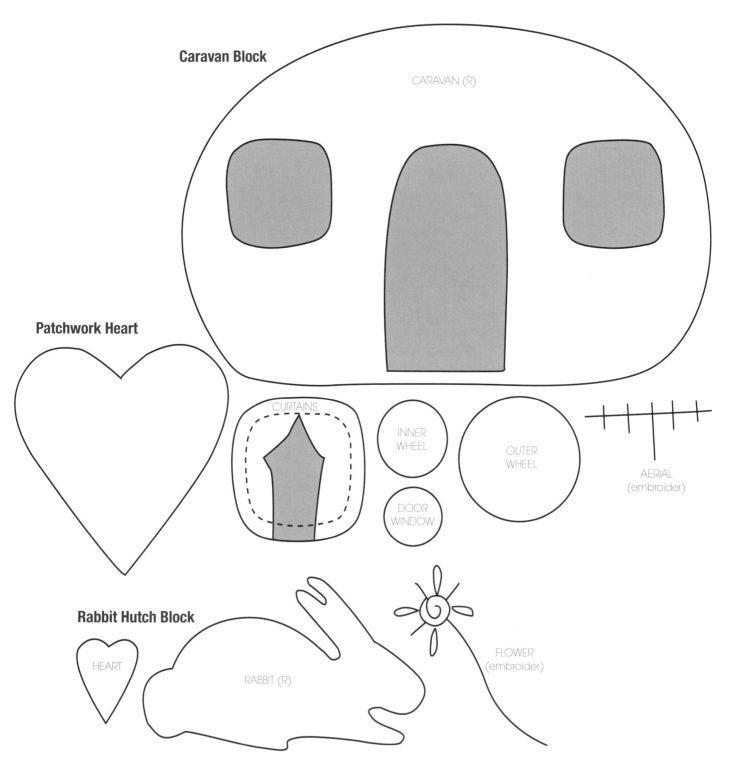

Caravan Block

CARAVAN (R)

Patchwork Heart

CURTAINS

INNER
WHEEL

OUTER
WHEEL

DOOR
WINDOW

AERIAL
(embroider)

Rabbit Hutch Block

HEART

RABBIT (R)

FLOWER
(embroider)

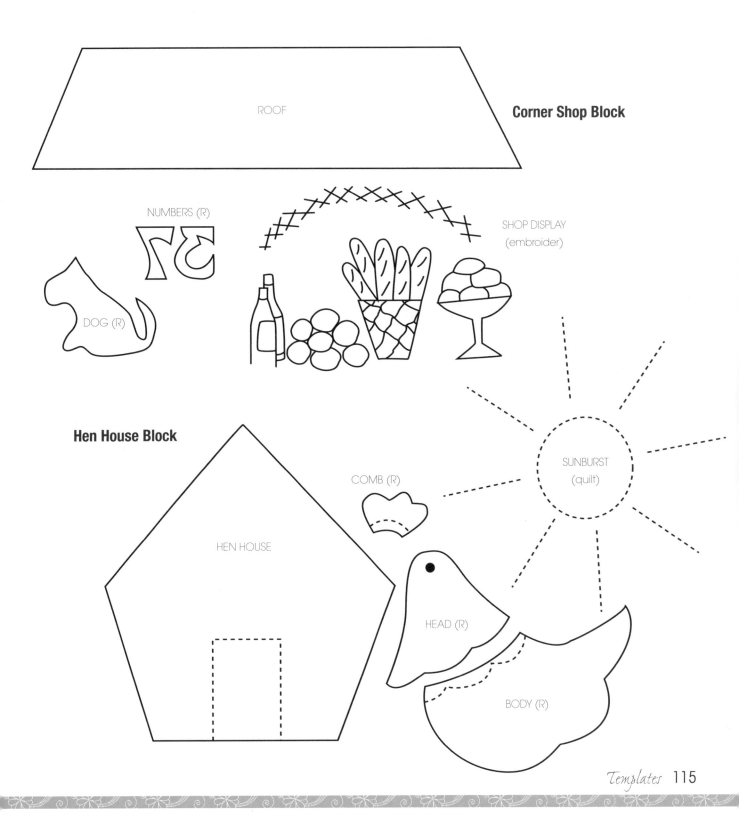

ROOF

Corner Shop Block

NUMBERS (R)

SHOP DISPLAY
(embroider)

DOG (R)

Hen House Block

COMB (R)

SUNBURST
(quilt)

HEN HOUSE

HEAD (R)

BODY (R)

Templates 115

Rose Cottage Block

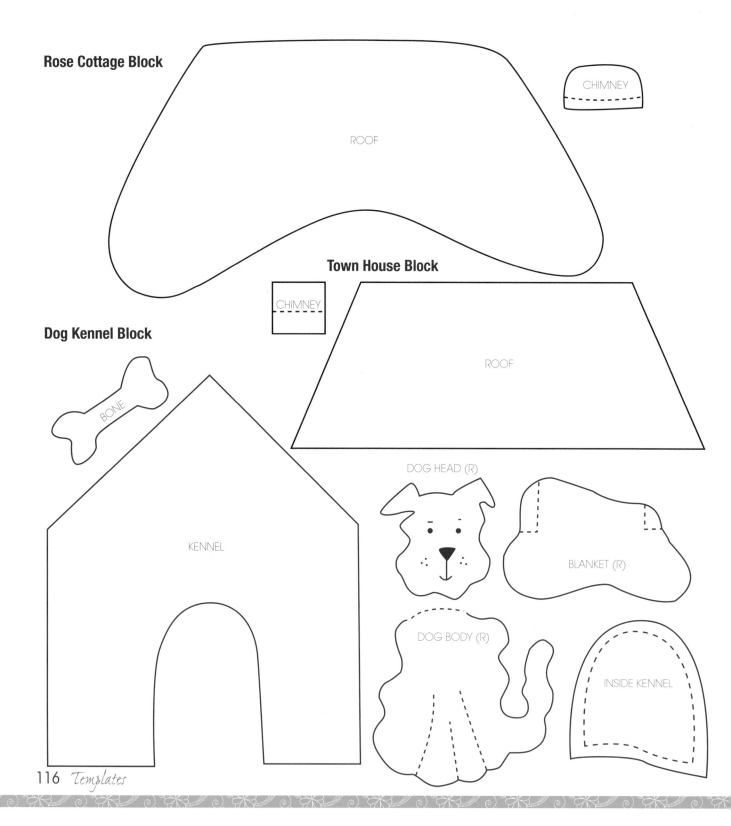

CHIMNEY

ROOF

Town House Block

CHIMNEY

ROOF

Dog Kennel Block

BONE

KENNEL

DOG HEAD (R)

BLANKET (R)

DOG BODY (R)

INSIDE KENNEL

Beach Hut Block

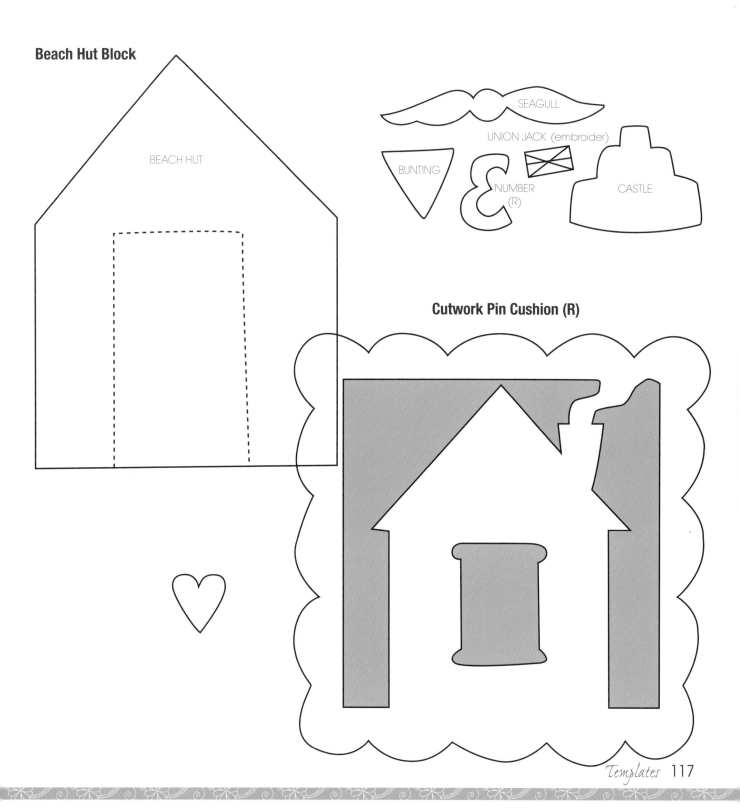

BEACH HUT

SEAGULL

UNION JACK (embroider)

BUNTING

NUMBER
(R)

CASTLE

Cutwork Pin Cushion (R)

Cutwork Cushions

HEART COTTAGE (R)

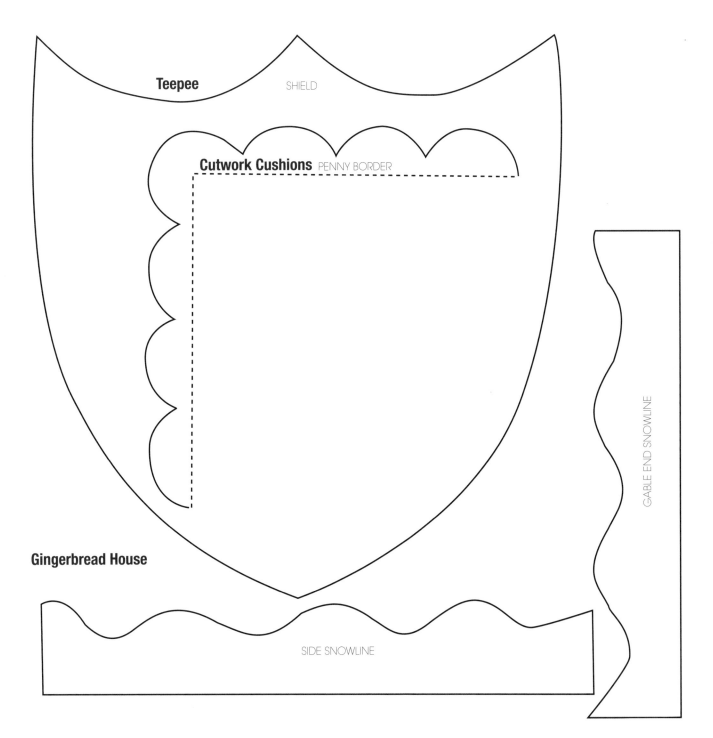

Teepee SHIELD

Cutwork Cushions PENNY BORDER

GABLE END SNOWLINE

Gingerbread House

SIDE SNOWLINE

Templates 121

Gingerbread House

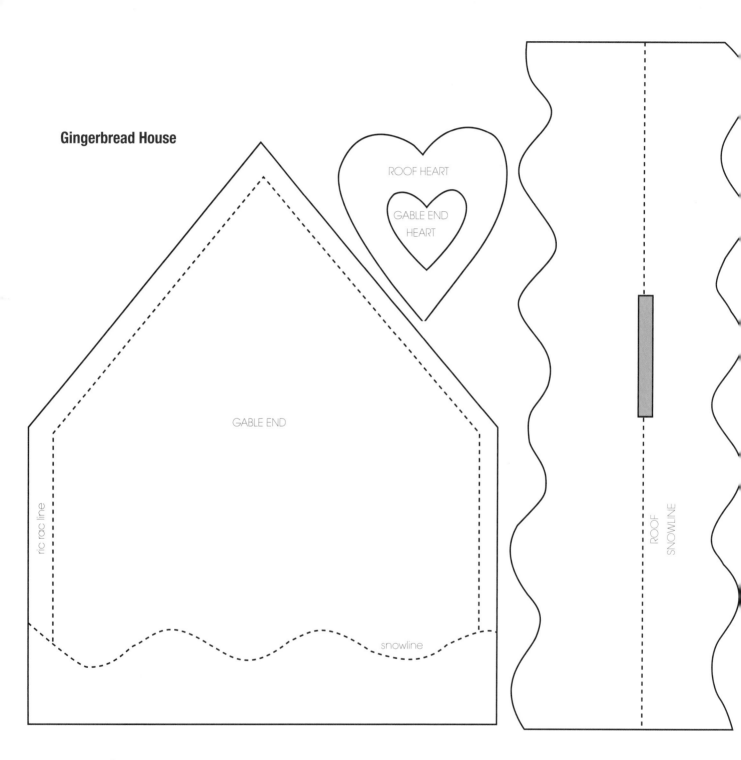

ROOF HEART

GABLE END
HEART

GABLE END

ric rac line

snowline

ROOF
SNOWLINE

Patterns

note: For those patterns that have been reproduced with a red outline, use the pattern to draw around the shape onto your fabric, and stitch on the drawn line BEFORE cutting out the shape close to the stitching line. This will result in a very accurate sewn shape and is great for awkward shapes and curves. (For your information, this type of pattern is more often referred to as a template in the sewing industry.) All other patterns are cut out and sewn with a 6mm (¼in) seam allowance unless otherwise specified in the project instructions, and all seam allowances have been added.

note: All patterns on this page have been reduced. For actual size increase by 200%.

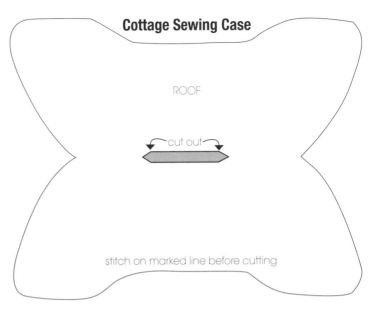

Cottage Sewing Case

ROOF

cut out

stitch on marked line before cutting

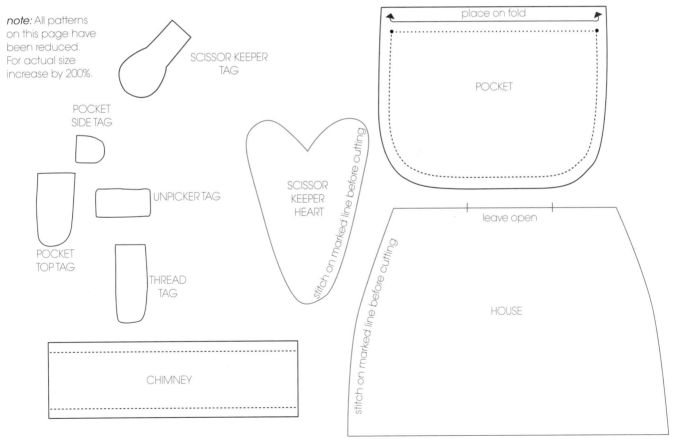

SCISSOR KEEPER TAG

POCKET SIDE TAG

UNPICKER TAG

POCKET TOP TAG

THREAD TAG

CHIMNEY

SCISSOR KEEPER HEART

stitch on marked line before cutting

place on fold

POCKET

leave open

stitch on marked line before cutting

HOUSE

Scruff Soft Toy

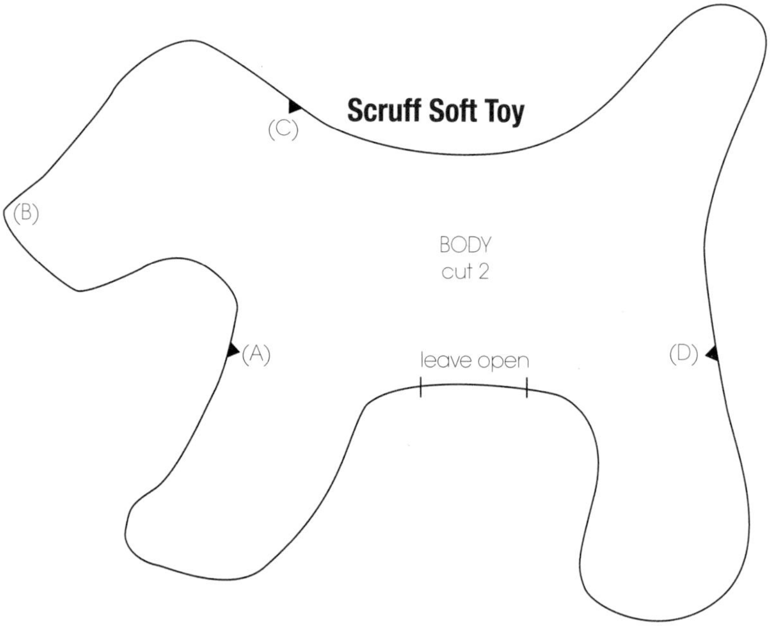

(C)

(B)

BODY
cut 2

(A)

leave open

(D)

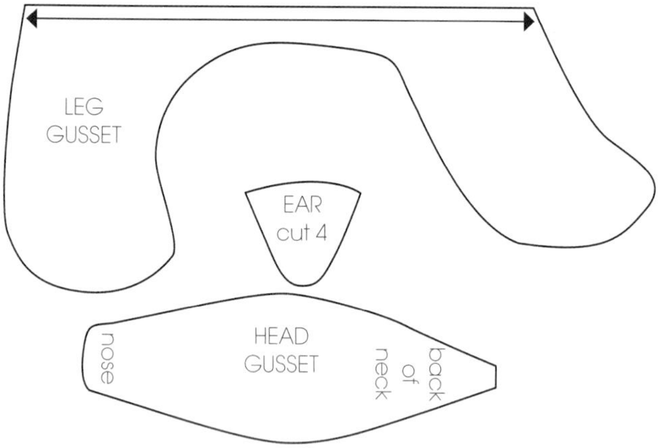

place on fold

LEG
GUSSET

EAR
cut 4

nose

HEAD
GUSSET

back
of
neck

Dog Neckerchief

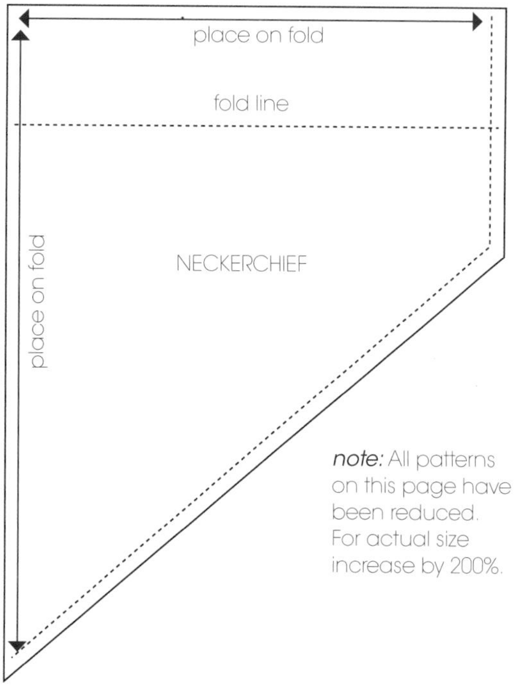

place on fold

fold line

place on fold

NECKERCHIEF

note: All patterns
on this page have
been reduced.
For actual size
increase by 200%.

Bunting

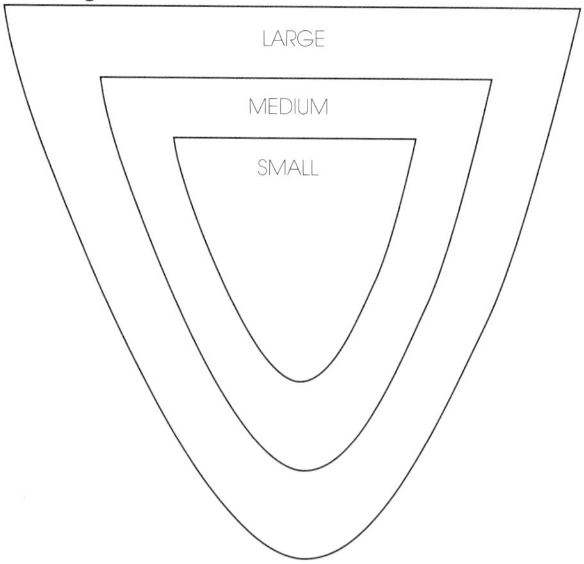

LARGE

MEDIUM

SMALL

Beach Bag

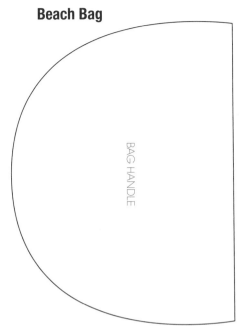

BAG HANDLE

note: The Bag Handle template has been reduced. For actual size increase by 200%.

Tree Decorations

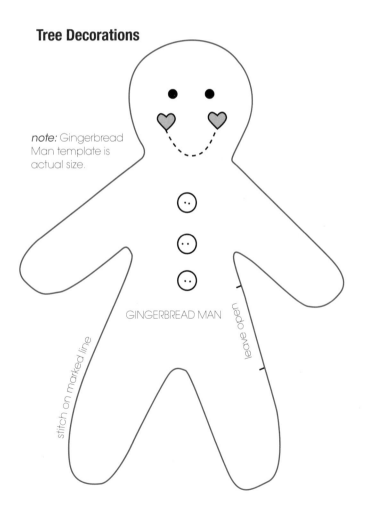

note: Gingerbread Man template is actual size.

GINGERBREAD MAN

stitch on marked line

leave open

Acknowledgments

I am very priviledged to have a wonderful network of friends, family and students that inspire me with endless enthusiam – my grateful thanks and love go to all of them. A very special mention goes to my sewing angel Jenny, who never lets me down, my husband Phil who yet again copes with dust, odd socks, copious amounts of quilts and very strange meals, and last but not least, baby Bertie who always makes me smile.

About the Author

Mandy Shaw describes herself as a maker of all things lovely and shares this passion with you all in this, her third book for David & Charles. She lives in East Sussex with her large family and travels all around the UK teaching and lecturing and attending the major quilt shows. She has appeared on Kirstie Allsopp's TV shows and contributed several projects to Kirstie's latest book. To find out more about Mandy's unique style visit www.dandeliondesigns.co.uk, where her patterns and wares can be bought.

Suppliers

Dandelion Designs
37 Summerheath Road, Hailsham,
East Sussex, BN27 3DS
www.dandeliondesigns.co.uk
Supplier of Mandy's patterns and kits and lots of fabric and haberdashery items related to Mandy's books including tapes, ric-rac, Fast2Fuse, felt, coton à broder and other threads.

The Patchwork Dog and Basket
The Needlemakers, West Street,
Lewes, East Sussex, BN27 2NZ
Tel: 01273 483886
www.patchworkdogandbasket.co.uk
For patchwork and quilting fabrics, buttons, tapes and haberdashery and workshops with Mandy.

The Cotton Patch
Tel: 0121 702 2840
www.cottonpatch.co.uk
For patchwork and quilting supplies.

Dunelm Mill
Tel: 0845 165 6565
www.dunelm-mill.com
For feather cushions and stuffing.

Deckchair Stripes
Tel: 01244 336387
www.deckchairstripes.co.uk
For deckchair canvas.

Index

Dedication

To my very first grandchild Bertie who I know is going to
give me so much inspiration for new makes.

A DAVID & CHARLES BOOK

© F&W Media International, LTD 2012

David & Charles is an imprint of F&W Media International, LTD
Brunel House, Forde Close, Newton Abbot, TQ12 4PU, UK

F&W Media International, LTD is a subsidiary of F+W Media, Inc.
4700 East Galbraith Road, Cincinnati, OH 45236

First published in the UK and USA in 2012
Digital edition published in 2012

Text and designs © Mandy Shaw 2012
Layout and photography © F&W Media International, LTD 2012

Names of manufacturers and product ranges are provided for
the information of readers, with no intention to infringe copyright
or trademarks.

A catalogue record for this book is available from the British Library.

ISBN-13: 978-1-4463-0168-5 paperback
ISBN-10: 1-4463-0168-0 paperback

ISBN-13: 978-1-4463-5579-4 e-pub
ISBN-10: 1-4463-5579-9 e-pub

ISBN-13: 978-1-4463-5578-7 PDF
ISBN-10: 1-4463-5578-0 PDF

Paperback edition printed in China by RR Donnelley
for F&W Media International, LTD
Brunel House, Forde Close, Newton Abbot, TQ12 4PU, UK

10 9 8 7 6 5 4 3 2 1

Publisher Alison Myer
Acquisitions Editor Katy Denny
Desk Editor Jeni Hennah
Project Editor Cheryl Brown
Senior Designer and Illustrator Mia Farrant
Photographers Vanessa Davies and Lorna Yabsley
Production Manager Beverley Richardson

David & Charles publish high quality books on a wide range of
subjects. For more great book ideas visit: www.rucraft.co.uk